T0196003

Topics in Multiphase Transport Phenomena

Robert W. Lyczkowski
Dimitri Gidaspow

authorHOUSE®

AuthorHouse™
1663 Liberty Drive
Bloomington, IN 47403
www.authorhouse.com
Phone: 1 (800) 839-8640

Published by AuthorHouse 01/17/2020

ISBN: 978-1-7283-4163-7 (sc)
ISBN: 978-1-7283-4162-0 (e)

Library of Congress Control Number: 2019921241

Print information available on the last page.

The authors wish to thank Dr. Wen Ho Lee for rekeying the equations in Chapters 1 and 2.

Contents

Preface ix

About the Authors xi

1. A Fluid-Porous Solid Reaction Model With Structural
   Changes 1

2. Kinetics of the Reaction of CO_2 With Solid K_2CO_3 39

3. Silicon Deposition Reactor Using High Voltage Heating 83

4. Alternative Methods of Deriving Multiphase Field
   Equations 109

Preface

Chapter 1 A Fluid-Porous Solid Reaction Model With Structural Changes, supplies details on modeling reactions with porous catalysts. The unique feature of this chapter is the pore closing, pore opening condition. This analysis is particularly useful for improving the design of storage batteries. Until the publication of "A Model for Discharge of Storage Batteries" by Dimitri Gidaspow and Bernard S. Baker, Journal of the Electrochemical Society,120, 1005-1010 (1973) the discharge of batteries was described by a purely empirical equation as a function of time. Chapter 2 Kinetics of the Reaction of CO_2 With Solid K_2CO_3, complements U.S. patent No. 3,865,924 (February 11,1975) by Dimitri Gidaspow and Michael Onischak, on rates of carbon dioxide (CO_2) capture. These rates of reaction were measured in a parallel plate channel at several laminar flow velocities. An integral equation flow analysis was used to obtain diffusion independent rates of reactions. Chapter 3 Silicon Deposition Reactor Using High Voltage Heating, describes an internally heated fluidized bed with no size limitations and with no bubble formation and its simulation. Chapter 4 Alternative Methods of Deriving Multiphase Field Equations, constitutes a literature review of approaches that have been used and/or proposed in the literature to derive multiphase flow equations which could form the basis of the theory and computation of dense suspensions of particulates such as coal-water slurries or blood flow.

About the Authors

Dimitri Gidaspow obtained his B.Ch.E. (cum laude) from the City College of New York, M.Ch.E. from the Polytechnic Institute of Brooklyn, and Ph.D. from the Illinois Institute of Technology (IIT). He is Distinguished Professor of Chemical Engineering, IIT (emeritus). Before joining IIT he was Adjunct Assistant Professor and then Full Professor at the Institute of Gas Technology (IGT). He is Principal Advisor of 65 Ph.D. students and many Masters students.

His Industrial experience began at Air Products. While at IGT he worked on (1) fuel cells, receiving an award from the Marshall Space Flight Center, and (2) desiccant air conditioning. In each of these fields he authored many peer-reviewed publications. He served as consultants for the Atomic Energy Commission (AEC) at Aerojet Nuclear Company in Idaho, Lawrence Livermore Laboratory, Energy Research Corp., Argonne National Laboratory, the Department of Energy, United Technology Corporation (UTC), EXXON, Westinghouse, Electric, Illinois Institute of Technology Research Institute (IITRI), MOBIL, UOP, and Polysilicon Corp.

His major professional activities_include Papers Chairman for AIChE Heat Transfer and Energy Conversion Division, Editor of "Heat Transfer- Research and Design" AIChE Heat Transfer Symposium Series Volume 70, No. 138 (1974), Program Chairman for the Intersociety Energy Conversion Engineering Conference and editor of a 2 volume set of proceedings for the American Chemical Society (ACS), Chairman of the AIChE multiphase flow committee (7g), Particle Technology Forum (PTC) chair at AIChE meetings, and multiphase computational fluid dynamics (CFD) tutorials.

He holds 10 US patents over 200 refereed publications (over 10,000 citations in Google Scholar). He is the author of four books: 1. Dimitri Gidaspow, "Multiphase Flow and Fluidization, Continuum and Kinetic Theory Description", Academic Press,1994. 2. Dimitri Gidaspow and Veeraya Jiradilok, " Computational Techniques. The Multiphase CFD Approach to Fluidization and Green Energy Technologies" Nova Science Publishers, 2009. 3. Hamid Arastoopour, Dimitri Gidaspow and Emad Abbasi, "Computational Transport Phenomena of Fluid-Particle Systems" Springer, 2016, and 4. H. Arastoopour, D. Gidaspow, and R. W. Lyczkowski, "Transport Phenomena in Multiphase Systems" Springer, in preparation 2020.

His awards include: AIChE Donald Q. Kern Award delivering the Lecture: "Hydrodynamics of Fluidization and Heat Transfer: Supercomputer Modeling", (Appl. Mech. Rev. 39, No. 1, 1-23, 1986), NSF Creativity Award, Fellow of the American Institute of Chemical Engineers, IIT Alumni awards, AIChE Flour-Daniel Lectureship Award in Fluidization., Ernst W. Thiele Award, Sigma Xi award., Thomas Baron award, Festschrift (I&EC Research, 49,No.11, June 2, 2010), and PTF award for lifetime achievements.

Robert W. Lyczkowski received his B.Ch.E in from Cleveland State University, Fenn School of Engineering and M.S. in Gas Engineering and Ph.D. in Gas Technology from Illinois Institute of Technology. He worked for Lawrence Livermore National Laboratory, Idaho National Engineering Laboratory, Energy Incorporated, Goodyear Atomic Corp., Hooker Chemical Corp., and as a faculty member at Illinois Institute of Technology. He has been involved for over forty years in chemical and nuclear engineering applications of his multiphase theory and computational fluid dynamics expertise especially in the areas of heat transfer and energy conversion to develop models that are now used by industry world-wide to design various two-phase flow equipment. He is a Fellow of the American Institute of Chemical Engineers and a recipient of the prestigious Ernst W. Thiele Award.

Most of Dr. Lyczkowski's career was spent as a Chemical Engineer in the Energy Systems Division at Argonne National Laboratory. He was involved with computer modeling of fluidized beds and dense slurries. His expertise is in the areas of multiphase flow and heat transfer, erosion, light water and liquid metal nuclear reactors, in-situ processing of fuels, and concentrated suspensions. He applied multiphase dense slurry modeling to the development of a unique non-Newtonian power-law model for multiphase hemodynamics. This established a completely new paradigm for analyzing the migration of blood-borne particulates. This model was used to develop a mechanistic monolayer population balance cell-adhesion model to aid in determining the threshold conditions of atherosclerosis initiation and progression. He was involved with modeling a novel multiphase concept involving chemical water splitting using high temperature steam bubbling into a bath of molten calcium bromide as the first step in the calcium-bromine (Ca-Br) cycle.

He is the author of over 150 technical publications (over 50 refereed journal articles and book contributions and over 100 conference papers), over 50 reports, and holds 2 U.S. patents. He contributed significantly to the development of the RETRAN and COMMIX computer programs. He has recently completed a book published by Springer titled "The History of Multiphase Science and Computational Fluid Dynamics a Personal Memoir" and is collaborating on H. Arastoopour, D. Gidaspow, and R. W. Lyczkowski, "Transport Phenomena in Multiphase Systems" Springer, in preparation 2020.

1

A Fluid-Porous Solid Reaction Model With Structural Changes

ABSTRACT

A continuum model for reaction of a fluid with a porous solid based on differential mass balances of the solid phases is proposed. It predicts the frequently observed exponential decrease of rates of these reactions with time. A dimensionless group involving a ratio of molar volumes of the solid phases governs the predicted cases of pore closing or pore opening upon reaction. This group and initial fractions of solid phases form a criterion which tells the designer when a pore will close leading to incomplete reactant utilization. For a high Thiele modulus the model predicts an optimum void fraction.

Analytical solutions for rates and conversions as a function of time are given for fully accessible cases and for a reaction whose rate is independent of fluid concentration. The case of a first order reaction leads to a highly non-linear boundary-initial value problem which is solved using techniques of functional analysis. Reaction thickness was found to decrease with time for the case when the pore ultimately closes. In other situations, it moved into the slab of the porous solid. A high-flux or suction effect present at high gas concentrations significantly increases the conversion of solid.

INTRODUCTION

Solid-fluid reactions in which the solid reactant is transformed into another chemical state form the basis of many chemical processes, such as the production of iron from iron ore, gas from coal and electricity from storage batteries. Reactions of gases with solids also promise to be important in air pollution control, such as in the limestone [1] or other processes [2] for removing sulphur dioxide from flue gases. In these applications the solids are frequently porous. Nonporous solids are desirable for prevention of chemical reaction, such as by corrosion, since solid diffusion is quite slow.

Fluid reactions with nonporous solids can be adequately described by the shrinking core models, as presented in standard texts on the subject by Levenspiel [3] and by Smith [4]. Oxidation of nickel spheres [5] is an example of where a shrinking core model adequately describes experimental data. For reduction of iron oxide [6] a shrinking core model was found to be adequate for large but not for small particles. For the reaction of sulphur dioxide with calcined limestone [1] shrinking core models were found not to be applicable. In the latter cases the reaction occurred not at an interface between the unreacted solid and the product layer but well into the volume of the solid reagent.

Ishida and Wen [7] pointed out the need for a new model to handle the case of porous solids. They called such a model a "homogeneous model". The homogeneous model describes the reaction of a fluid within a porous solid with diffusion taking place through the solid reagent having a constant diffusivity. After all the solid reactant at the surface of the particle has been converted to a solid product, diffusion across the growing product layer was included. Apparently for mathematical simplicity the reaction was assumed to be independent of solid concentration. This led to a rate in stage one that was independent of time. However, rates of solid-fluid reactions with a consumable reagent are known to be time dependent from the beginning of reaction. Many of these reactions can be described as being first order with respect to some solid concentration, since they show an exponential decrease with time. For example, combustion of carbonaceous deposits within catalyst particles was first order with respect to carbon [8].

In the hydroflourination of uranium dioxide (UO_2) no boundary was found to exist between the solid reagent, UO_2, and the solid product, UF_4, and the rate was found to be directly proportional to the fraction of unreacted uranium dioxide [9]. Decomposition and reduction of iron pyrite were found to be first order with respect to FeS_2 in the early stages of the reaction [10]. Later pore closing was observed, which probably accounted for the differences. Data for the reaction of SO_2 with an activated manganese oxide were fitted to a first order mechanism [11]. Sorption of water by various hydrates was also first order with respect to the salt [12]. Hydration of magnesium oxide in water was also found to be first order [13], although a shrinking core mechanism was suggested but not proved in the paper. Coal char hydrogasification data indicate that the rate of carbon conversion in the first phase reaction is proportional to the amount of unreacted carbon [14]. In a principally theoretical study, a first order reaction with respect to a solid reactant was also used [15]. However, no structural changes of the solid were considered. The unsteady behavior was due to the change of solid concentration with time.

In this chapter it is shown that the first order behavior with respect to the solid reactant is a result of conservation of mass. The decrease of reactive material with time together with structural changes that begin immediately upon reaction are responsible for the variation of the rates with time.

The analysis applies to porous solids. In the continuum approximation used in this paper the porous solid may be viewed as consisting of an aggregate of fine particles, as shown in electron photo-micrographs [16]. Although diffusion in each of the primary particles may be in the solid phase, the Thiele modulus will still be small enough for each fine particle to be uniformly accessible. For example, in making porous electrodes for storage batteries [17, 18] great care is taken to prevent the formation of large crystals which will not contribute to the capacity of the storage battery.

BALANCES ON SOLID PHASES

Consider a solid-fluid reaction

$$\gamma_A A(f) + S(s) \rightarrow \gamma P(s) \tag{1}$$

where S is a solid reagent, P an insoluble solid product formed and the reactant A is in the fluid phase. The stoichiometric coefficient, γ_A, can be positive or negative and assume the values $\gamma_A = a, b, c, ...$ for several components participating in the reaction. At some time t, a volume element of cross sectional area A and width Δx contains the following phases: (1) solid reagent S, (2) solid product P, (3) a fluid phase filling the pores of the solid, and (4) an inert, such as a binder or support or both. On an inert free basis, let ε_s be the volume fraction of solid reagent S, ε_p be the volume fraction of the solid product P and let ε be the volume fraction of the fluid.

The mass balance on an element $A\Delta x$ for the solid reagent S is:

$$\frac{d}{dt}\int_x^{x+\Delta x} \rho_S A\varepsilon_s\, dx + \rho_S v_S \varepsilon_s]_x^{x+\Delta x} - \int_x^{x+\Delta x} r_V \varepsilon_s A\, dx, \tag{2}$$

where the first term on the left-hand side is the rate of accumulation of S, the second term the net rate of outflow of S out of the volume element by expansion, contraction, or diffusion and the term on the right is the mass rate of consumption of S. The symbols are defined in the Notation section. Note that r_V is the rate of consumption of S per unit volume of S. It makes no sense to express the rate per unit volume of total mixture, since reaction can occur only where there is reagent S present. The reaction does not occur in the fraction of space filled by the product, nor does it occur in the fluid phase. Hence the definition of rate above and the appearance of ε_s on the right side of Eq. (2). Application of mean value theorems to Eq. (2), shrinking of Δx to zero, assuming coexistent continua for the dispersed phases, yields the partial differential equation

$$A\frac{\partial(\rho_S \varepsilon_S)}{\partial t} + \frac{\partial(A\rho_S v_S \varepsilon_S)}{\partial x} = -r_V \varepsilon_S A, \tag{2a}$$

The density ρ_S is a unique property of the solid phase S which is only a function of thermodynamic variables, such as pressure and temperature. For plane geometry A is a constant and can be canceled in Eq. (2). For negligible solid diffusion, no overall expansion or contraction upon reaction v_S is zero. With local expansion taking place upon reaction with mass addition rate, r_V can be zero in a porous material since the solid will at first occupy the voids originally filled by the fluid. If necessary, in such a case, this restraint may be achieved by containing the reagent between two plates by force. Thus, for zero v_S and constant ρ_S we obtain the simple differential equation

$$\rho_S \frac{\partial \varepsilon_S}{\partial t} = -r_V \varepsilon_S, \tag{3}$$

and we assign an initial reagent distribution, ε_{S0}, as

$$\varepsilon_S(0) = \varepsilon_{S0}. \tag{4}$$

Eq. (3) is reminiscent of the frequently observed [8-15] first-order kinetic law in solid-gas reactions which is usually written as

$$\frac{dC_S}{dt} = -k_S C_S, \tag{5}$$

where the solid concentration C_S replaces ε_S and the first order rate constant k_S is simply r_V / ρ_S. Clearly, such a kinetic law can be simply a result of the mass balance as given by Eq. (3). No postulate of a kinetic mechanism is necessary. According to the above interpretation, if the reaction were to occur in solution, liquid, or solid, then we would obtain the zero-order law for the species S

$$\frac{dC_S}{dt} = -r_0. \tag{6}$$

In Eq. (6) it is reasonable to express the rate, r_0, per unit total volume, since reaction occurs all over.

Proceeding with the analysis, we see that integration of Eq. (3) with initial condition (4) gives the volume fraction of solid reagent ε_S as

$$\varepsilon_S = \varepsilon_{S0} \exp(-\frac{1}{\rho_S} \int_0^t r_V dt) . \tag{7}$$

The rate must, in general, be kept inside the integral sign in Eq. (7), because r_V is a function of concentration of the species in the fluid phase. Since the species in the fluid phase may have to diffuse from the surroundings into the porous solid, the concentration will in general be different from point to point in the porous solid.

The mass balance on the solid product P for a volume element $A\Delta x$ gives

$$\frac{d}{dt} \int_x^{x+\Delta x} \rho_P A \varepsilon_P dx + A\rho_P v_P \varepsilon_P]_x^{x+\Delta x} = \int_x^{x+\Delta x} \frac{r_V \gamma M_P}{M_S} \varepsilon_P A dx , \tag{8}$$

where stoichiometry shows that the rate of production of solid P is $r_V \gamma M_P / M_S$.

Again, for no overall expansion or contraction and no solid diffusion, v_P is zero and we obtain

$$\rho_P \frac{\partial \varepsilon_P}{\partial t} = \frac{r_V \gamma M_P}{M_S} \varepsilon_P , \tag{9}$$

with some initial distribution of P

$$\varepsilon_P(0) = \varepsilon_{P0} . \tag{10}$$

Integration of Eq. (9) gives

$$\varepsilon_P = \varepsilon_{P0} + \frac{\gamma M_P \varepsilon_{S0}}{M_S \rho_P} \int_0^t [r_V \exp(-\frac{1}{\rho_S} \int_0^t r_V dt] dt , \tag{11}$$

where in general $r_V = r_V(t,x)$ through its dependence on concentration of A.

Since we assumed the porous solid does not expand or contract, the fraction of the fluid phase, ε is obtained by difference as

$$\varepsilon = 1 - \varepsilon_S - \varepsilon_P . \tag{12}$$

COMPLETELY ACCESSIBLE REAGENT

If the diffusional gradient into the porous solid, as gas, measured by the Thiele modulus [4,19] is small or if the reaction is zero order with respect to the fluid concentrations, Eq. (7) becomes

$$\varepsilon_S = \varepsilon_{S0} e^{-\frac{r_V t}{\rho_S}} . \tag{13}$$

The rate of reaction for a porous solid of volume V_0 is then $V_0 \varepsilon_S r_V$. The rate of reaction per unit bulk volume is therefore

$$R_V = \varepsilon_{S0} r_V e^{-\frac{r_V t}{\rho_S}} . \tag{14}$$

The weight of S reacted per unit bulk volume up to time t is, by integration of Eq. (14)

$$W = \varepsilon_{S0} \rho_S (1 - e^{-\frac{r_V t}{\rho_S}}) . \tag{15}$$

We note that the rate of reaction and conversion are time dependent and that they decrease exponentially with time. Most rates of reaction of this type show this basic exponentially decreasing time dependence [8-15]. This basic unsteady observed phenomenon is sometimes used as a defense of shrinking core models, since they have an unsteady behavior built into them [4]. For the reaction-controlled case the cause of the unsteady behavior is the decrease of surface area with time. For the diffusion-controlled case, the cause of the time dependence is the continued build-up of an impervious product layer. Note that in the case of reasonably small particles and reactions of a solid with a gas, the product must be completely nonporous to offer an appreciable diffusion resistance. For example, J. M. Smith [4] obtains a diffusivity six orders of magnitude higher than the molecular gas diffusivity. The cause of the unsteady behavior in this model is the decrease of the fraction of reagent with time. We add that at least in one system [9], surface area measurements with fraction of reagent converted have shown that after surface area has ceased to vary with time after 25 percent conversion, the rate still continued to drop with time. Hence, it is clear that the simple model proposed should find wide application in process industries, where porous solid reagents are commonly used.

Eq. (14) shows that only at small times, $(r_V t / \rho_S) << 1$ will we measure the true rate of reaction. At higher times, rates will be masked due to conversion of the reagent. Consider the explicit example of a first-order reaction, such as occurs in the case of the carbonate reaction [20]

$$K_2CO_3(s) + H_2O + CO_2(g) \rightarrow 2KHCO_3(s) \qquad (16)$$

or in the case of the hydrofluorination of uranium dioxide [9]

$$UO_2 + 4HF \rightarrow UF_4 + 2H_2O . \qquad (17)$$

For reaction Eq. (17) it is stated that photomicrographs showed that it occurred uniformly throughout the particles. We have a first order dependence with respect to the concentration of CO_2 in Eq. (16) and a first order dependence with respect to hydrogen fluoride in Eq. (17). Then the molar rate of reaction becomes

$$\frac{r_V}{M_S} = k_c C_A , \qquad (18)$$

where C_A refers to the concentration of CO_2 or HF in the gas phase. The rate per unit volume, R_V ,

$$R_V = \varepsilon_{SO} M_S k_c C_A \exp(-k_c M_S C_A t / \rho_S) , \qquad (19)$$

has a maximum with concentration of C_A at large times. It will appear to be first order only initially and give a false lower order if calculated at some sufficiently large times only.

PORE CLOSING CONDITION

Under completely accessible conditions or for a zero-order reaction the mass balances for the solid reagent S and for the solid product P can be integrated independent of the equations for diffusion of fluid species, as shown for S in the previous section. In addition, these equations can be integrated at the pore mouth of a particle or slab of porous material, where the concentration can be maintained constant by, for example, flow of fluid containing the reactive species. The interfacial concentration can be computed using mass transfer coefficients in complex systems [4] or by exact methods in hydrodynamically well-defined situations [21-23]. Then the volume fraction of product ε_P becomes, using Eq. (11)

$$\varepsilon_P = \varepsilon_{P0} + \frac{\gamma M_P \rho_S \varepsilon_{S0}}{M_S \rho_P}[1 - \exp(-\frac{r_V t}{\rho_S})] \tag{20}$$

Call the ratio of molar densities and the stoichiometric coefficient γ an expansion factor, E

$$E = \frac{\gamma M_P \rho_S}{M_S \rho_P}, \tag{21}$$

since according to Eq. (20) it represents a fractional increase in volume of the solid phase. Then since all expansion or contraction occurs at the expense of the fluid phase filling the pores of the solid, we obtain the fraction of fluid phase from Eq. (12) as

$$\varepsilon = 1 - \varepsilon_{P0} - E\varepsilon_{S0} + \varepsilon_{S0}(E-1)\rho^{-\frac{r_V t}{\rho_s}}. \tag{22}$$

Differentiation of Eq. (22) with respect to t shows that we have the following three possibilities:

For $E > 1$, ε decreases with t monotonically
For $E = 1$, ε is invariant with time
For $E < 1$, ε increases with t monotonically
For the reaction of fluid + solid $\rightarrow$ solid (for example, Eq. (16), E

will normally be greater than one, since $\gamma M_P > M_S$. For the reverse reaction or for decomposition reactions $E < 1$.

For the case of expansion, $E < 1$ we have another restraint. The volume fraction of fluid cannot be negative. When we set ε to be equal to zero, we find that this occurs at some dimensionless time $\bar{t}_m$ equal to

$$\bar{t}_m = \frac{t_m r_V}{\rho_S} = \ln \frac{\varepsilon_{SO}(E-1)}{(\varepsilon_{PO} + E\varepsilon_{SO} - 1)} \, . \qquad (23)$$

When $E > 1$ and $(\varepsilon_{PO} + E\varepsilon_{SO}) > 1$, the pore will close at some time, t_m after the start of the reaction, given by Eq. (23). After this maximum time, t_m, diffusion will have to take place across an impervious layer of product or "ash" as it is frequently called. In a completely accessible situation, the pore will close uniformly. When the rate of reaction is a monotonically increasing function of concentration of a controlling species in the fluid, the pore will close at its mouth first. Then the reaction will be in a second stage, as illustrated by Ishida and Wen [7]. Only in this model diffusion equations have to be solved simultaneously with the balances for the solid phases, resulting in a system of partial differential equations and not in the system of ordinary differential equations solved by Ishida and Wen.

For the pore never to close, let t be infinite in Eq. (22) and use the restraint $\varepsilon \geq 0$. This gives the useful relation

$$(\varepsilon_{PO} + E\varepsilon_{SO}) \leq 1 \, . \qquad (24)$$

This relation limits the fraction of solid reagent that a porous reactant should be made of. Thus, we should never use a pure crystalline reagent as a reactant when it forms a solid product with $E > 1$, if we want it to be completely effective. Instead relation Eq. (24) dictates that it should for example, be dispersed on some support that has sufficient voids to accomodate the increase in mass upon reaction. Relation Eq. (24) shows that it is not sufficient to start out with a reagent of merely very large surface area.

Before concluding this section, it may be of interest to point out that pore plugging has been observed and qualitatively described in the literature. Schwab and Philinis [10] in their study of the reactions of iron pyrite attribute incomplete conversion to pore closing. Vinal [17] discusses it in connection with the discharge of sulfuric acid lead storage batteries. Lead sulfate, which is formed as a product of the discharge of the cells, is known to be less dense than either lead or lead dioxide. It therefore occupies more space than the active materials and blocks the pores, resulting in a lowered capacity of the battery. Soda [24], in an investigation supervised by the author, studied the reaction of CO_2 with a 1/16 inch layer of pressed K_2CO_3, as given by Eq. (16), at room temperature at various CO_2 compositions. He found that at first rates dropped with time approximately exponentially, but near 5 percent theoretical K_2CO_3 conversion, they appeared to decrease to zero more than an order of magnitude more rapidly. This was particularly evident for high CO_2 concentrations, where rates were initially higher. Later the salt was dispersed on a porous support and complete. conversion to bicarbonate was achieved at high CO_2 concentrations extremely rapidly [20].

When the pore closes under uniformly accessible conditions, that is when the Thiele modulus is very small for the system, the weight of solid reagent that has reacted is given by Eq. (15) with t equal to $\bar{t}_m$. This maximum time, $\bar{t}_m$, is given by Eq. (23). Substitution of Eq. (23) into Eq. (15) gives

$$W_\infty = \frac{\rho_S(1-\varepsilon_{SO}-\varepsilon_{PO})}{(E-1)}. \tag{25}$$

Expression Eq. (25) is interpreted as the final weight of S reacted per unit bulk volume, $W_\circ$, assuming the diffusivity through the product layer is negligibly small. This final weight depends only upon the structural parameters of the initial porous solid and on the expansion factor E. It is, of course, valid only when inequality Eq. (24) is violated.

WITH VOLUME CHANGES

Consider the diffusionally fully accessible particle or a collection of particles examined previously but now allow overall volume changes. Since there is no concentration change into the particles, we make an overall balance over the system. The material balance for S gives:

$$\frac{d}{dt}(V\varepsilon_P\rho_P) = \frac{r_V\gamma M_P}{M_S}\varepsilon_S V V\varepsilon_P = (V\varepsilon_P)_0 + E(V\varepsilon_S)_0(1-e^{-r_W t}), \tag{26}$$

where V is the volume of all the particles. Integration using $(V\varepsilon_S)_0$ the initial condition again gives the exponential drop with time. The rate for the. system expressed in say, grams of S reacted per second, is

$$R = (V\varepsilon_S)_0 e^{-\frac{r_V t}{\rho_S}} . \tag{27}$$

Rate experiments generally give R as expressed above. For scaling purposes, it is useful to express the rate per unit mass of S. This gives

$$R_W = \frac{(V\varepsilon_S)_0 r_V}{W_S} e^{-\frac{r_V t}{\rho_S}} = \frac{r_V}{\rho_S} e^{-\frac{r_V t}{\rho_S}} , \tag{28}$$

where W_S is the total weight of S in the sample and it is recognized that' ρ_S is the ratio of W_S to $(V\varepsilon_S)_0$. The initial rate that we measure is then r_V / ρ_S. If we call this r_W then the rate at any time in terms of quantities measured becomes

$$R_W = r_W e^{-r_W t} . \tag{29}$$

Since experimentalists generally try to make measurements on fully accessible systems, it is not surprising that relation Eq. (29) holds for so many practical fluid-solid reactions [8-15, 20].

Again, the volume of the solid product' on a pore-free basis can be obtained from a material balance. The mass balance of P over all particles in the system under investigation is:

$$\frac{d}{dt}(V\varepsilon_P\rho_P) = \frac{r_V\gamma M_P}{M_S}\varepsilon_S V . \tag{30}$$

Integration using $(V\varepsilon_P)_0$ as the initial condition gives the volume of crystalline product

$$V\varepsilon_P = (V\varepsilon_P)_0 + E(V\varepsilon_S)_0(1-e^{-r_W t}) . \tag{31}$$

If somehow the fluid fraction, ε remained constant, then Eq. (31) shows that the factor E is an overall measure of expansion or contraction. However, it appears that unless we assume V to be a constant, ε must in general be calculated from a momentum balance taking into account the solid mechanics of the system.

WITH DIFFUSION AT CONSTANT PRESSURE

The molar balance for the fluid reactant A, in Eq. (1), with a variable fluid fraction, ε, is

$$A\frac{\partial(C_A\varepsilon)}{\partial t} + \frac{\partial(C_A v_A A\varepsilon)}{\partial x} = -\frac{r_V \gamma_A \varepsilon_S A}{M_S}. \tag{32}$$

For the inert in the gas phase, called component B, we have the equation

$$A\frac{\partial(C_B\varepsilon)}{\partial t} + \frac{\partial(C_B v_B A\varepsilon)}{\partial x} = 0. \tag{33}$$

The usual [25] definitions $C = C_A + C_B$ and $Cv^* = C_A v_A + C_B v_B$ give the continuity equation in molar units

$$A\frac{\partial(C\varepsilon)}{\partial t} + \frac{\partial(C_B v^* A\varepsilon)}{\partial x} = -\frac{\gamma_A r_V}{M_S} A\varepsilon_S. \tag{34}$$

As noted earlier γ_A can represent a sum of stoichiometric coefficients over A. Thus for equimolar diffusion the right side of Eq. (34) will be zero.

From the ideal gas law, we see that at constant temperature and pressure, C is a constant. Then C can be taken outside the differentiation operation in Eq. (34). Under these conditions using Fick's law of diffusion

$$Y_A(v_A - v^*) = -D\frac{\partial Y_A}{\partial x}, \tag{35}$$

where Y_A is the mole fraction of species A, the molar balance for species A becomes

$$\varepsilon \frac{\partial Y_A}{\partial t} + \varepsilon v^* \frac{\partial Y_A}{\partial x} - \frac{1}{A}\frac{\partial}{\partial x}(A\varepsilon D \frac{\partial Y_A}{\partial x}) = -\frac{\gamma_A r_V \varepsilon_S}{M_S C}(1 - Y_A). \qquad (36)$$

In Eq. (36) the velocity v^* is determined by Eq. (34). It can be obtained by simple quadrature when the partial with respect to ε can be neglected compared with the other terms in the equation.

For equimolar diffusion or dilute mixtures v^*, as always, is zero. It is interesting to observe that Eq. (36) is a diffusion equation with a time dependent and concentration dependent diffusion coefficient εD. Experimental fits of sorption data to a diffusion equation often give a diffusion coefficient which is time and/or concentration dependent [26].

DILUTE ZERO ORDER REACTION

For plane geometry, a dilute fluid mixture in component A and a rate independent of concentration a simple analytical solution can be obtained.

The diffusion equation Eq. (36) becomes

$$\frac{d}{dx}(\varepsilon D \frac{dY_A}{dx}) = \frac{\gamma_A r_0 \varepsilon_S}{M_S C}, \qquad (37)$$

where r_0 is now the zero-order rate. The fraction of solid reagent, ε_S, is given by Eq. (13) and ε by Eq. (22). This simplification implies that S reacts independent of the presence of A. The usual boundary conditions (B. C.'s) for a zero-order reaction are

B. C. 1: $Y_A(0) = Y_0$, B. C. 2: $\dfrac{dY_A(L)}{dx} = 0$, B. C. 3: $Y_A(L) = 0$, $\qquad (38)$

which state that we have a prescribed concentration at zero x and no A left to react after some length L which is assumed to be sufficiently large. This reaction thickness, L becomes

$$L = \left[\frac{2Y_0 C M_s D}{\gamma_A r_0}(\frac{\varepsilon}{\varepsilon_S}) \right]^{1/2}. \qquad (39)$$

As in catalysis, this reaction thickness varies directly with the square root of pore mouth concentration and diffusivity. The new feature is that the reaction thickness is time dependent. This follows from the examination of the ratio $\varepsilon / \varepsilon_S$ which is

$$\frac{\varepsilon}{\varepsilon_S} = (1 - \varepsilon_{PO} - E\varepsilon_{SO})e^{\frac{r_0 t}{\rho_S}} / \varepsilon_{SO} + (E-1). \tag{40}$$

When the pore never closes, that is when $(\varepsilon_{PO} + E\varepsilon_{SO}) < 1$, this reaction thickness or penetration depth increases with time indefinitely. This means, as the solid reagent is consumed near the pore entrance at $x = 0$, the gas has to diffuse further and further into the particle to find reactive material. When the pore closes, $(\varepsilon_{PO} + E\varepsilon_{SO}) > 1$, L decreases to zero at time $\bar{t}_m$. This occurs because the effective diffusion coefficient εD vanishes as ε goes to zero. The relation also says that for non-porous materials, that is for zero void fraction, we will not have any penetration into the solid by diffusion in the fluid phase, as expected. Note that the very slow diffusion through the solid phase has been neglected at this stage of the problem.

The observed rate per unit visible area A is equal to the flux at zero x. In the fully accessible case this rate may be obtained by multiplying the rate per unit volume R_V by the thickness, L. In this case the measured rate per unit volume will depend upon the thickness of the slab of porous material that we start with. It is therefore best to talk of the rate per unit visible area, R_{mA}. In electrochemical applications this is essentially the current density. We have

$$R_{mA} = -\varepsilon DC \frac{dY_A(0)}{dx} = \left[\frac{2Y_0 \gamma_A r_0 \varepsilon_S \varepsilon CD}{M_S} \right]^{\frac{1}{2}}, \tag{41}$$

or

$$R_{mA} = e^{-\frac{r_0 t}{2\rho_S}} \left\{ (\frac{2Y_0 \gamma_A r_0 \varepsilon_S \varepsilon CD}{M_S})[(1 - \varepsilon_{PO} - E\varepsilon_{SO}) + \varepsilon_{SO}(E-1)e^{-\frac{r_0 t}{2\rho_S}}] \right\}^{\frac{1}{2}} \tag{41a}$$

.

In Eq. (40) we note the occurrence of the product of volume fractions of the solid reagent and of the fluid. This gives rise to an optimum void fraction. Specifically, consider the case of no product P initially and zero time. Then the rate, R_A is proportional to

$$\varepsilon_S \varepsilon = \varepsilon_{SO} - \varepsilon_{SO}^2,\qquad(42)$$

which gives

$$\text{optimum } \varepsilon_{SO} = 0.5,\qquad(43)$$

for highest initial rate.

It is worthy to remark that Vinal [17] recommends that porous electrodes for for storage batteries have a 50% porosity. Although no mathematical analysis of the type performed here is yet available for storage batteries [18], the coincidence of these numbers is not accidental, since in a storage battery with a high metal conductivity $Y_A C$ in Eq. (37) would be replaced by polarization and D by electrical conductivity of the electrolyte. This somewhat unrelated problem is mentioned here, because the author is not aware of any similar recipes for preparing porous solids used in the process industries. We also note that the 50 percent porosity is both job and model dependent.

The product of the fractions of solid reagent and of the fluid in Eqs. (40) and (41) also leads to two types of behavior with time. We recall that ε_S is always a decreasing function with time, while ε is a decreasing function of time for $E > 1$ but an increasing function for $E < 1$. Thus, when the pore tends to close upon reaction, the rate will decrease with time, as expected. However, when $E < 1$ the rate may increase at first and then decrease, since at first the rate may increase due to better accessibility but then must drop due to consumption of the reagent. The case of pore opening generally occurs in decomposition reactions. Analysis of Eq. (41) shows that if the initial fraction of solid reagent is not large, such that

$$\varepsilon_{SO} < \frac{1 - \varepsilon_{PO}}{2 - E}, \text{ for } E < 1\qquad(44)$$

the rate will decrease with time initially also and not go through a maximum. Suppose ε_{PO} is zero and E is 0. 5, then the rate will decrease with time unless $\varepsilon_{SO} > 0.67$.

In computing the weight of fluid species A reacted, and in quantitatively using Eqs. (39) through (41) for times significantly larger than zero, one must keep in mind the zero-order assumption made in Eq. (37). As stated, it was assumed that S is consumed at a constant rate independent of the fluid concentration. This implies that when beyond the length L, the concentration of A is zero, S still keeps disappearing at a rate that depends on elapsed time only. When L decreases with time, there is no problem. However, when L increases with time, the fluid reactant A begins to contact an already partially consumed solid reagent and the analysis is of no physical interest. Thus, for the case of $\varepsilon_{PO} + E\varepsilon_{SO} > 1$ the weight of fluid A that reacted from zero to time t per unit visible area is

$$W_A = \int_0^t R_{mA} dt .$$ (45)

Integration using Eq. (41) gives the dimensionless weight of A reacted

$$\bar{W}_A = \frac{W_A}{\rho_S \left[2\gamma_A \varepsilon_{SO} Y_0 CD / (M_S r_0) \right]^{\frac{1}{2}}},$$ (46)

as a function of dimensionless time $\bar{t} = (t / \rho_S) r_0$ as

$$\bar{W}_A = \sqrt{f_1 + f_2} + \frac{f_1}{\sqrt{f_2}} \ln[\sqrt{f_2} + \sqrt{f_1 + f_2}]$$

$$- e^{\frac{-\bar{t}}{2}} \sqrt{f_1 + f_2 e^{-\bar{t}}} - \frac{f_1}{\sqrt{f_2}} \ln[e^{\frac{-\bar{t}}{2}} \sqrt{f_2} + \sqrt{f_1 + f_2 e^{-\bar{t}}}] ,$$ (47)

valid for $\varepsilon_{PO} + E\varepsilon_{SO} > 1$ and $0 " \bar{t} " \bar{t}_m$ where

$$f_1 = (1 - \varepsilon_{PO} - E\varepsilon_{SO}) ,$$ (48)

$$f_2 = \varepsilon_{SO}(E - 1) ,$$ (49)

and $\bar{t}_m$ is given by Eq. (23). When the pore closes completely the final weight of A that has reacted per unit area become

$$W_{A\infty} = \rho_S \left[\frac{2\gamma_A \varepsilon_{SO} Y_0 CD}{M_S r_0}\right]^{\frac{1}{2}} [(1 - \varepsilon_{PO} - \varepsilon_{SO})^{\frac{1}{2}}$$

$$-(\varepsilon_{PO} + E\varepsilon_{SO} - 1)(\varepsilon_{SO})^{-\frac{1}{2}}(E - 1)^{-\frac{1}{2}} \ln \frac{(\varepsilon_{SO})^{\frac{1}{2}}(E-1)^{\frac{1}{2}}+(1-\varepsilon_{PO}-\varepsilon_{SO})^{\frac{1}{2}}}{(\varepsilon_{PO}+E\varepsilon_{SO}-1)^{\frac{1}{2}}}], \qquad (50)$$

for $\varepsilon_{PO} + E\varepsilon_{SO} > 1$.

When $\varepsilon_{PO} + E\varepsilon_{SO}$ approaches unity, L' Hospital's rule shows that the long second term in brackets in Equation (50) vanishes. We also see that as ε_{SO} approaches unity, the weight of A reacted approaches zero.

Eq. (50) gives two physically interesting conclusions that are not obvious. The first is that the final weight reacted is proportional to the square root of concentration of the species A in the fluid. Such a reduced capacity of a sorbent at low gas concentrations is usually attributed to thermodynamic equilibrium, as expressed by, say, Freundlich or Langmuir-type isotherms [27]. Although this is frequently the case, this model provides an alternate explanation that may be useful for interpreting some anomalies as observed in the half-order reaction of SO_2 with activated manganese oxide [11]. The authors of that study observed that the final conversion is a function of operating conditions which unfortunately not detailed. The second interesting conclusion is that the final capacity is inversely proportional to the square root of the intrinsic rate of reaction. Thus, higher intrinsic rates of reaction lead to poorer utilization of the reagent in the case of large particles. This observation may be useful in, say, selecting the best alkali carbonate for sorbing carbon dioxide. The most reactive carbonate may not be the one needed. The formula also says that if the rate increases with temperature, utilization of the reagent will be poorer at higher temperatures. We also observe that for large particles and rapid reactions, the reaction zone will be limited to a narrow outside shell. Then after the time t, diffusion will have to proceed through a compacted material. In this regime shrinking core models should be approximately applicable. This may be why shrinking core models sometimes are valid for large particles, but not for sufficiently small particles [6].

FIRST ORDER REACTION

The diluteness assumption, the usual pseudo-steady state approximation [28] and the use of the first order kinetic law as expressed by Eq. (18) lead to the following diffusion equation

$$\frac{\partial}{\partial x}(\varepsilon \frac{\partial Y}{\partial x}) = \varphi^2 Y \varepsilon_S,$$ (51)

where φ is the usual Thiele modulus

$$\varphi = L\sqrt{\frac{\gamma_A k_C}{D}},$$ (52)

and the distance is put in non-dimensional form using the half length of the slab of porous material as the scale factor. With a prescribed concentration at the pore mouth we have the boundary conditions

B. C. 1: $Y(t,0) = 1$, B. C. 2: $\dfrac{\partial Y(t,1)}{\partial x} = 0$. (53)

The characteristic time for the system is $\rho_S / (M_S Y_0 C k_C)$ which is used to obtain the dimensionless time in

$$\varepsilon_S = \varepsilon_{SO} \exp[-\int_0^T Y d\bar{t}].$$ (54)

The void fraction $\varepsilon = 1 - \varepsilon_S - \varepsilon_P$ is obtained using Eqs. (54) and (9) as

$$\varepsilon = (1 - E\varepsilon_{SO} - \varepsilon_{PO}) + (E-1)\varepsilon_S.$$ (55)

The mathematical task is one of solving a highly nonlinear initial-boundary value problem in two independent variables.

The molar rate of reaction of A per unit visible area is the rate of diffusion through the pores

$$R_{mA} = -DC\varepsilon(t,0)\frac{\partial Y_A(t,0)}{\partial x}, \tag{56}$$

or the integral of the rate of consumption of S

$$R_{mA} = \gamma_A k_C C \int_0^L \varepsilon_S Y_A dx. \tag{57}$$

When the pore is completely accessible, Eq. (57) becomes

$$R_{mA} = L\varepsilon_{SO}\gamma_A k_C CY_A e^{-t}. \tag{58}$$

It is related to the rate per unit volume in Eq. (19) through the length L and the molecular weight. Eq. (58) gives us a proper scale factor for rate. It is the rate at zero time for pure S. Thus, define the dimensionless molar rate of reaction of A as

$$\bar{R}_{mS} = \frac{R_{mA}}{\gamma_A k_C Y_0 CL\varepsilon_{SO}}. \tag{59}$$

This dimensionless rate is a sort of an effectiveness factor. Eqs. (56) and (57) give, respectively

$$\bar{R}_{mS} = -\frac{1}{\varphi^2}\frac{\varepsilon(\bar{t},0)}{\varepsilon_{SO}}\frac{\partial Y(\bar{t},0)}{\partial \bar{x}}, \tag{60}$$

$$\bar{R}_{mS} = \frac{1}{\varepsilon_{SO}}\int_0^L Y\varepsilon_S d\bar{x}. \tag{61}$$

As the Thiele modulus, φ approaches zero, Eq. (60) yields an indeterminate form, since the gradient is zero and φ is zero. The second form of the rate gives $\exp(-\bar{t})$ which is the fully accessible expression for the dimensionless rate.

The weight fraction reacted up to time t is

$$\bar{W} = \frac{W_A}{\dfrac{M_A\gamma_A L\rho_S\varepsilon_{SO}}{M_S}} = \int_0^L \bar{R}_{mS}d\bar{t}. \tag{62}$$

In Eq. (62) W_A is the weight of A reacted per unit visible area. It is scaled by $\rho_S\varepsilon_{SO}L$ which is the weight of S present initially per unit area s so multiplied by the stoichiometric conversion factor

$\gamma_a M_A / M_S$ that converts S to A. Therefore, the dimensionless weight of A, $\bar{W}$, is also the weight fraction of the reagent S reacted. When the pore does not close, as required by inequality Eq. (24), at infinite time $\bar{W}$ approaches one. When the pore closes $\bar{t}$ in Eq. (62) ranges from zero to $\bar{t}_m$, with $\bar{t}_m$ given by Eq. (23). We note that for the dilute first-order reaction considered, the final weight reacted is not a function of concentration of A. It is a function of $\varepsilon_{SO}, \varepsilon_{PO}, E$, and φ. As the Thiele modulus is made very small, it is anticipated that in the limits as $\varphi^2 \to 0$ and $\bar{t} \to \bar{t}_m$, we obtain

$$\bar{W} = \frac{1 - \varepsilon_{SO} - \varepsilon_{PO}}{\varepsilon_{SO}(e-1)}. \tag{63}$$

This was found to be true computationally.

Integral Equation and Marching

Integration of Eq. (51) with the two boundary conditions given by Eq. (53) yields the nonlinear integral equation

$$Y(\bar{t}, \bar{x}) = 1 + \varphi^2 \int_0^{\bar{x}} \frac{dz}{\varepsilon} \int_0^z Y\varepsilon_S dx' - \varphi^2 \int_0^{\bar{x}} \frac{dz}{\varepsilon} \int_0^1 Y\varepsilon_S dx'. \tag{64}$$

At every time, $\bar{t}$ the above integral equation can be solved by improved iteration [29]. The integrals were approximated by the trapezoidal quadrature formula. Up to a Thiele modulus squared of ten, it is sufficient to divide the interval zero to one into fifty parts.

The following improved iteration scheme was found to be useful from the point of view of programming and computer time. Eq. (64) is a functional equation of the form

$$Y = G(Y). \tag{65}$$

The Newton-Raphson-Kantorowitch method gives

$$Y_{n+1} = Y_n - \frac{Y_n - D(Y_n)}{1 - DG(Y_n)}, \tag{66}$$

where the subscripts denote the iterate and DG is the Frechet derivative of the operator G. DG can be approximated at every iterate by the usual quotient of differences' as for instance in the reguli falsi method. In such an approximation of a derivative the integral in Eq. (64) must be evaluated twice. Instead a crude approximation for DG was obtained by disregarding the Y dependence on ε_S while differentiating the integrals in Eq. (64). Thus, DG becomes roughly the distribution for a zero-order reaction. Taking out mean values of ε_S and ε we obtain

$$DG = \frac{\varphi^2 \overline{\varepsilon}_S \overline{x}^2}{2\overline{\varepsilon}} - \frac{\overline{\varphi^2 \varepsilon_S \overline{x}}}{\overline{\varepsilon}}. \tag{67}$$

This type of improved iteration proved very effective, except when the pore was about to close. Convergence to four significant figures was achieved in as few as two iterations for small time increments.

Equation (54) allows marching of the solution in time. When the integral, for small time increments, is approximated by the trapezoidal formula, we obtain

$$\varepsilon_S(\Delta \overline{t}, \overline{x}) = \varepsilon_S(0, \overline{x}) \exp\left[-\frac{\Delta \overline{t}}{2} Y(0, \overline{x}) \right] \exp\left[-\frac{\Delta \overline{t}}{2} Y(\Delta \overline{t}, \overline{x}) \right]. \tag{68}$$

At zero time $\varepsilon_S(0, \overline{x})$ is ε_{SO} and $Y(0, \overline{x})$ is computed using Eq. (64) so or an analytic solution. At time $\Delta \overline{t}$, ε_S depends implicitly on $Y(\Delta \overline{t}, \overline{x})$ as seen from Eq. (68). At this time $\varepsilon_S(\Delta \overline{t}, \overline{x})$ is the ε_S in Eq. (64). We know it once the integral equation Eq. (64) is solved. Then for the. next time interval this new value of ε_S becomes the initial value $\varepsilon_S(0, \overline{x})$ for every $\overline{x}$. Simultaneously, ε in Eq. (64) is computed using Eq. (55). Time increments were chosen to be sufficiently small to meet accuracy rather than the less stringent expected stability requirement. Stability problems were encountered only when an attempt was made to calculate the void fraction using Eqs. (11) and (12), rather than Eq. (55). As an initial guess for Y at time $\overline{t}$ greater than zero, the computed distribution at time $(\overline{t} - \Delta \overline{t})$ was used. Since for small time increments the Y distribution differed little from the one from the previous time increment, convergence of the integral equation scheme was extremely rapid in most cases.

NUMERICAL RESULTS

Zero order rate analysis already indicated that we expect radically different behavior between the case when solid reactant can be completely reacted and the case when the pore closes and unreacted material is trapped inside a shell. For zero ε_{P0} and for E of 1. 5, the pore will stay open upon completion of reaction if $\varepsilon_{S0} = 0.5$, while it will close at a dimensionless time of 0.69 if $\varepsilon_{S0} = 0.8$, according to the criterion given by Eq. (24).A few selected computational results are presented graphically for these two cases. Fig. 1.1 shows the void fraction distribution at various times for the two cases for a Thiele modulus square of ten. The upper five curves refer to the ease when the void distribution decreases from 50 percent to 25 percent at the completion of the reaction. Since the void fraction is, by a material balance, algebraically related to the fraction of solid reagent S reacted, the graphs show how the reaction eats its way into the slab of reactant. This shows the trend predicted by the zero order reaction analysis. With such a high Thiele modulus, most of the reaction occurs first near the surface. As the reactant near the surface is consumed, the reaction moves into the depth of the slab. With a Thiele modulus of one or lower, the pore closes at a nearly uniform rate all throughout the slab. The lower three curves show how the void fraction distribution changes from a uniform 20 percent value to the distribution at near pore closing for the case when solid reagent is trapped inside a hard crust.

Fig. 1.2 shows some typical concentration profiles for the two distinctly different situations. For the case when the pore does not close completely the top curves show how the fluid concentration changes with time from an initially non-uniform distribution to a more and more uniform profile. The curves are actually for the case when the diluteness assumption has been lifted, but the behavior is the same. The lower curves, (a) and (b) are for the previously discussed pore closing situation. The concentration profile becomes steeper with time as the pore closing condition is approached.

The dimensionless rate of reaction or a kind of an effectiveness factor is plotted in Fig. 1.3 as a function of time for the pore closing case. The rate drops to zero sharply near a value of dimensionless time of 0.69 and the process changes over to diffusion through a product layer which has not been calculated. The numerical results presented show two characteristics which were not obvious from analysis alone. The first. is that even for large Thiele moduli, the rate is an exponentially decreasing function of time up to reasonably large conversions, since the numbers generated can be fitted to a straight line on the semilogarithmic paper. Thus, the mere fact that data can be fitted to a first order solid concentration law is not enough to guarantee freedom from diffusional corrections. For example, the effectiveness factor is about 15 percent and less for the case of Thiele modulus square of ten. However, we also see that the slopes for all the curves are very close to the fully accesible case. Thus, rate constants obtained from such slopes should be nearly free of diffusional effects, while rate constants obtained from data extrapolated to zero solid reactant conversion will be in great error. In view of these numerical results, it is suggested that the applicability of Eq. (29) be used as a test of fully accessible reaction. When the intrinsic rates obtained from the slope and from the intercept are the same, the data are free of diffusional effects.

The fraction of solid reactant converted to solid product is plotted as a function of dimensionless time in Fig. 1.4 for the previously discussed pore closing case. For a given physico-chemical system, the parametric values of the square of the Thiele moduli can be interpreted as slab thicknesses or particle radii. Borgwardt [1], for example, shows curves of the shape of Fig. 1.4 for sorption of sulfur dioxide by different particles of dolomite for apparently short reaction times. Fig. 1.4 also shows how the final fraction of solid reagent reacted at the dimensionless time of 0. 69 varies with the Thiele modulus. Even a φ^2 of 0.01 does not completely give the limiting value of the final fraction of 0. 5. A φ^2 of 10 already corresponds to such a large particle that only about 6 percent of the solid reagent will react before the process goes over into the much slower combined diffusion across the growing product layer.

HIGH GAS CONCENTRATIONS

At high gas concentrations the fluid reactant A will enter the pores by both diffusion and by convection due to the suction effect created by a reduction in volume upon reaction. For a constant molar density, C, first-order rate given by Eq. (18), and with the usual pseudo-steady state approximation, Eq. (34) determines the dimensionless velocity or Peclet number by means of the following equations:

$$\frac{\partial (P_e \varepsilon)}{\partial \bar{x}} = -\varphi^2 Y_0 Y \varepsilon_S,\tag{69}$$

and

$$P_e(\bar{t},1) = 0.\tag{70}$$

The convective diffusion equation is

$$\frac{\partial (P_e \varepsilon)}{\partial \bar{x}} - \frac{\partial}{\partial \bar{x}}(\varepsilon \frac{\partial Y}{\partial \bar{x}}) = -\varphi^2 Y \varepsilon_S,\tag{71}$$

with the boundary conditions given by Eq. (53) and ε_S determined by Eq. (54). Integration of the above equations gives the integral equation for, the concentration of species A as

$$Y(\bar{t},\bar{x}) = 1 + \varphi^2 \int_0^{\bar{x}} \frac{(1-Y_0 Y)dz}{\varepsilon} \int_0^z Y \varepsilon_S dx' - \varphi^2 \int_0^{\bar{x}} \frac{(1-Y_0 Y)dz}{\varepsilon} \int_0^1 Y \varepsilon_S dx'.\tag{72}$$

Amazingly in this form Eq. (72) differs very little from Eq. (64) for the case of zero convection. Only minor changes in the program were needed to numerically solve this problem. The dimensionless rate is still given by Eq. (61) and the weight fraction reacted by Eq. (62). In this case, however, the final weight fraction is a function of the concentration of the reactive species A in the fluid phase. The mole fraction at the surface of the slab, Y_0, is an additional parameter in the dimensionless representation.

With convection the concentration does not decrease as rapidly into the slab, as seen from curve (c) in Fig. 1.2. The effect of suction is to give the appearance of a higher diffusion coefficient. However, as in similar high flux problems, this effect is not important at small concentrations of say 5 percent or less. Fig. 1.5 shows the effect of concentration on the weight fraction of the solid reactant converted to solid product. For on 80 percent fluid mixture, the conversion is nearly twice that obtained with no suction. Such gradually increasing final conversions were obtained for the reaction of pure, pressed potassium carbonate with carbon dioxide and water [24]. Large reductions in pressure caused by the decrease of volume upon reaction have also been measured when finely dispersed hydrated potassium carbonate is suddenly exposed to pure carbon dioxide in a flask. Such experiments demonstrate the importance of including convective diffusion at high gas concentrations.

ACKNOWLEDGMENT

This work was carried out as part of the basic research program of the Institute of Gas Technology.

NOMENCLATURE

A = cross sectional area of porous solid, cm^2, also refers to reactive component A in the fluid phase

B = refers to unreactive component B in the fluid phase

C = molar density of fluid, $C_A + C_B$

C_A = molar concentration of reactant A in the fluid phase, mole A/cm^3 fluid

C_B = molar concentration of inert in the fluid phase, mole B/cm^3 fluid

C_S = conventional solid concentration of S

D = effective diffusivity of A in the fluid phase of the porous solid, cm^2/s

E = expansion factor involving a ratio of molar volumes, $\gamma M_P \rho_S / M_S \rho_P$

k_c = first- order rate constant as defined in Eq. (18), (mole S/cm^3 S-s)/ (mole $A/cm^3 A$)

L = half-thickness of a slab of porous material in first order reaction analysis, cm; also reaction thickness in Eq. (39) for a zero-order reaction

M_P = molecular weight of P, gP/mole P

M_S = molecular weight of S, gS/mole S

P_e = dimensionless velocity or Peclet number, $v^* L / D$

r_0 = zero-order rate of consumption of S in Eq. (37), gS/cm^3 S-s

r_V = mass rate of consumption of solid S per unit volume of S, gS/cm^3 S-s

r_W = intrinsic mass rate of consumption of S, s^{-1}, ρ_S/r_V

R = measured rate of reaction, gS/s

R_V = measured rate of reaction per unit total volume, gS/cm^3 total-s

R_W = measured mass rate of consumption of S per unit weight of S, s^{-1}

R_{mA} = molar rate of consumption of species A per unit visible area, mole A/cm^2-s

$\overline{R}_{mS}$ = dimensionless rate or effectiveness factor with respect to the rate at zero time as defined by Eq. (59)

t = time, s

t_m = time at which the pore closes, s

$\overline{t}$ = dimensionless time, tr_V / ρ_S

v_A = velocity of species A in the fluid phase, cm/s

v_P = contraction velocity of solid product P, cm/s

v_S = contraction velocity of solid S, cm/s

v^* = molar average velocity in the fluid phase, cm/s

V = bulk volume of solid, cm^3

W = weight of S reacted per unit bulk volume, gS/cm^3 total

W_A = weight of A reacted, expressed in moles, per unit visible area, mole A/cm^2

$W_{A°}$ = weight of A reacted at pore closing with a zero order reaction, moles A / cm^2

$W_°$ = final weight of S reacted per unit bulk volume, gS / cm^3 total

W_S = weight of solid reactant S, g

$\overline{W}_A$ = dimensionless weight of A reacted with a zero-order reaction as defined by Eq. (46)

$\overline{W}$ = weight fraction of solid reacted

x = space coordinate in the direction of pores, cm

$\overline{x}$ = dimensionless length, x / L

x' = integration variable related to $\overline{x}$

Y = dimensionless concentration of species A in the fluid, Y_A / Y_0

Y_A = mole fraction of reacting species A in the fluid phase

Y_0 = mole fraction of component A at zero x

z = integration variable related to $\overline{x}$

GREEK LETTERS

γ = stoichiometric coefficient in Eq. (1), mole $P/$ mole S

γ_A = stoichiometric coefficient in Eq. (1), moles $A /$ mole S

ε = void fraction, cm^3 fluid/cm^3 total

ε_p = volume fraction of solid product P, cm^3 P/ cm^3 total

ε_{P0} = initial volume fraction of solid product P, cm^3 P/cm^3 total

ε_S = volume fraction of solid reactant S, cm^3 S / cm^3 total

ε_{S0} = initial volume fraction of solid reactant S, cm^3 S/ cm^3 total

$\bar{\varepsilon}$ = average volume fraction of solid reactant from zero to $\bar{x}$

$\bar{\bar{\varepsilon}}_S$ = average volume fraction of solid reactant from zero to one

$\bar{\varepsilon}$ = average void fraction from zero to $\bar{x}$

ρ_P = void free density of solid product P , g P/cm^3 P

ρ_S = void-free density of solid S , g S/cm^3 S

φ = Thiele modulus, $L\sqrt{\dfrac{\gamma_A k_c}{D}}$

REFERENCES

1. Borgwardt, R. H. "Kinetics of Reaction of SO_2 with Calcined Limestone", Environmental Sci. and Tech. 4, No. 1, 59-63 (1970)
2. U. S. Department of Health, Education and Welfare, National Air Pollution Control Administration No. AP-52, "Control Techniques for Sulfur Oxide Air Pollutants", January 1969

3. Levenspiel, Octave, "Chemical Reaction Engineering", John Wiley, New York (1962)

4. Smith, J. M. "Chemical Engineering Kinetics", McGraw-Hill, New York (1970)

5. Carter, R. E. "Kinetic Model for Solid-State Reactions", J. Chem. Phys. 34, No. 6, 2010-15 (1961)

6. Themelis, N. J. and Gauvin, W. H., "Reduction of Iron Oxide in Gas Conveyed Systems", AIChE Journal 8, 437-444 (1962)

7. Ishida, M. and Wen, C. Y., "Comparison of Kinetic and Diffusional Models for Gas-solid Reactions", AIChE Journal 14, 311-17 (1968)

8. Weisz, P. B. and Goodwin, R. B., "Combustion of Carbonaceous Deposits within Porous Catalyst Particles. II. Intrinsic Burning Rate", J. Catalysis 6, 227-235 (1966)

9. Tomlinson, L., Morrow, S. A., and Graves, S., "Kinetics of Hydrofluorination of Uranium Dioxide", Trans. Faraday Soc. 57, 1008-18 (1961

10. Schwab, M. G. and Philinig, John, "Reactions of Iron Pyrite: Its Thermal Decomposition, Reduction by Hydrogen and Air Oxidation", J. Am. Chem. Soc. 69, 2588-96 (1947)

11. Uno, T., Fakui, M., Atsukawa, M., Higashi, M., Yamada, H., and Kamei, K., "Scale-up of a SO_2 Control Process", Chem. Eng. Progress 66, No. 1, 61-66 (1970)

12. Punwani, Dharamvir, Chi, C. W., and Wasan, D. T., "Dynamic Sorption by Hygroscopic Salts," I&EC Process Design and Development 7, 410-15 (1968)

13. Smithson, G. L. and Bakhshi, N. N., "The Kinetics and Mechanism of Hydration of Magnesium Oxide in a Batch Reactor", Can. J. Chem. Eng. 47, 508-13 (1969)

14. Wen, C. Y. and Huebler, J., "Kinetic Study of Coal Char Hydrogasification", I&EC Process Design and Development 4, 142-47 (1965)

15. Lacey, D. T., Bowen, J. H., and Basden, K. S., "Theory of Noncatalytic Gas-Solid Reactions", I&EC Fundamentals 4, 275-81 (1965)
16. Terence, Allen, "Particle Size Measurement", Chapman and Hall, London (1968)
17. Vinal, G. W., "Storage Batteries", John Wiley, New York (1951)
18. Jasinski, Raymond, "High Energy Batteries", Plenum Press, New York (1967)
19. Satterfield, C. N. and Sherwood, T. K., "The Role of Diffusion in Catalysis," Addison-Wesley, Reading (1963)
20. Onischak, Michael and Gidaspow, Dimitri "Separation of Gaseous Mixtures by Regenerative Sorption on Porous Solids Part II. Regenerative Separation Of CO_2", p. 71-93 in "Recent Developments in Separation Science," Vol. II, Chemical Rubber Co., Cleveland, Ohio (1972)
21. Gidaspow, Dimitri, "Green's Functions for the Graetz Problem and Interfacial Concentrations", AIChE Journal 17, 19-24 (1971)
22. Solbrig, C. W. and Gidaspow, Dimitri, "Turbulent Mass-Transfer with an Arbitrary Order Surface Reaction in a Flat Duct", Int. J. Heat Mass-Transfer 11, 155-180 (1968)
23. Kulacki, F. A. and Gidaspow, Dimitri, "Convective Diffusion in a Parallel Plate Duct with One Catalytic Wall- Laminar Flow-First Order Reaction, Part Il. Experimental", Can. J. Chem. Eng. 45, 72-8, (1967)
24. Soda, Kunihisa, "Regenerative Sorption of CO_2" Master of Science in Gas Engineering Thesis, June 1969, Illinois Institute of Technology.
25. Bird, R. B., Stewart, W. E., and Lightfoot, E. N., "Transport Phenomena", John Wiley, New York (1960)
26. Crank, J. "The Mathematics of Diffusion", Oxford University Press, Oxford (1956)

27. Marcusen, Lis, "The Kinetics of Water Adsorption on Porous Alumina", <u>Chem. Eng. Science 25</u>, 1487-99 (1970)
28. Wen, C. Y. "Noncatalytic Heterogeneous Solid Fluid Reaction Models", I&EC, 60, 34-54 (1968)
29. Collatz, Lothar, "Functional Analysis and Numerical Mathematics", Academic Press, New York (1966)

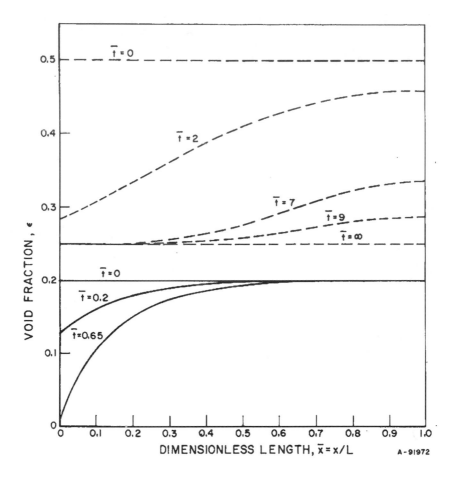

Fig. 1.1. Void fraction distributions with a large diffusional resistance at several times for: (a) ultimate complete solid conversion with ε_{SO} = 0.5 – dashed curves (b) incomplete solid utilization with ε_{SO} = 0.8 – solid curves. Dilute first order reaction. ε_{PO} = 0, E = 1.5, φ = 10

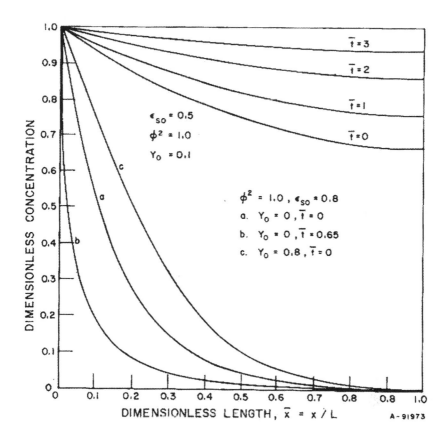

Fig. 1.2. Typical fluid concentration distributions for cases of complete (top curves) and incomplete (bottom 3 curves) solid reactant utilization at various times

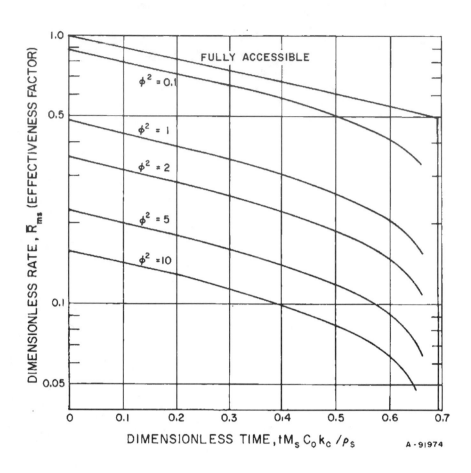

Fig. 1.3. Effect of Thiele modulus on rate of a dilute first order reaction with ultimate solid reactant utilization for $\varepsilon_{PO} = 0$, $E = 1.5$, $\varepsilon_{SO} = 0.8$

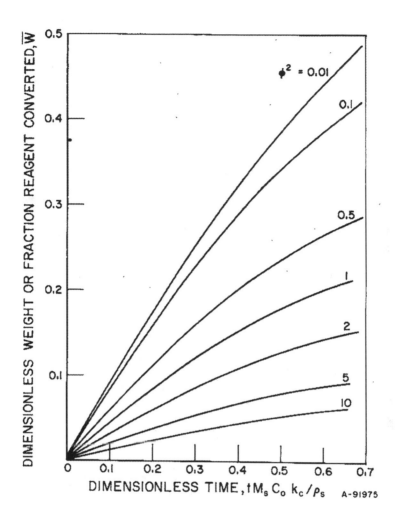

Fig. 1.4. Effect of Thiele modulus on the fraction of solid reactant converted for a dilute first order reaction for $\varepsilon_{PO} = 0$, E = 1.5, $\varepsilon_{SO} = 0.8$

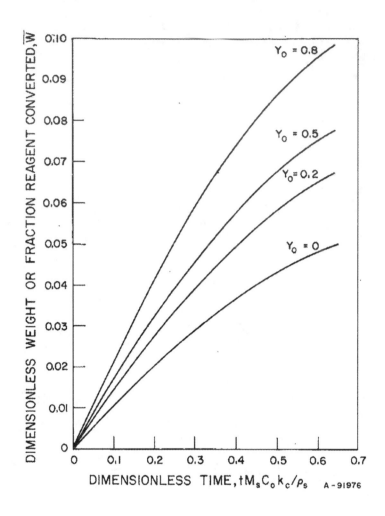

Fig. 1.5. Effect of high fluid mole fractions on solid reactant utilization. First order reaction. $\varepsilon_{PO} = 0$, $E = 1.5$, $\varepsilon_{SO} = 0.8$, $\varphi^2 = 10$

2

Kinetics of the Reaction of CO_2 With Solid K_2CO_3

ABSTRACT

Rates of reaction of CO_2 with hydrated K_2CO_3, both in the pure state and dispersed on fine alumina, were studied in an isothermal parallel plate reactor as a function of time, concentration of CO_2 in the range of 0.5 to 20 percent, and temperature. The dispersed sorbent was regenerated thermally without a loss in activity. Rates were calculated both from thermal regeneration of the bicarbonate and by using an integral equation analysis for the Graetz problem.

The rate of reaction for the dispersed sorbent, in terms of grams K_2CO_3 converted per 'gram of K_2CO_3 initially present per hour, is at room temperature,

$$\text{rate} = 3.5x_{CO_2} \exp[-(3.5x_{CO_2} + 2.3)t] \tag{1}$$

where x_{CO_2} is mole percent CO_2 and t is time in hours. The formula is valid until about 70 percent conversion. Rates calculated from extrapolation to zero time and from a variation with time show that the conventional effectiveness factor for a porous solid is one for the dispersed carbonate. The effectiveness factor for the pure salt is low and varies with CO_2 concentration. These observations are in agreement with a fluid-porous solid model developed earlier. Data could not be satisfactorily explained by shrinking core and other conventional models.

The removal of CO_2 from a gas stream is a common industrial operation [1, 2, 3]. However, commercial scrubbers are too large for use in many potential appliances for example such as those involving molten carbonate or base fuel cells. Also as pointed out by Weber, Miller and Gregor [4], in environmental control applications, such as in submarines and space vehicles, the present practices are inadequate for some missions. For example, lithium hydroxide scrubbers [5] used in space vehicles or sealabs [6] are of non-regenerative type. Due to these needs a number of studies were carried out recently using solid reagents that can be regenerated [4, 7, 8].

Our potential sorption — regeneration device has to meet the following requirements set by the sponsor of this study: 1) It has to be smaller than a molten carbonate fuel cell [9], 2) CO_2 must be transferred from water saturated streams, 3) Regeneration must be accomplished using waste heat, and, 4) Sorption and regeneration must occur at atmospheric pressure. The CO_2 transfer problem is particularly difficult in the case of the molten carbonate fuel cell, because reforming of methane produces a carbon dioxide-hydrogen mixture which is fed to the anode, where the hydrogen reacts. It is, however, at the cathode, where CO_2 is needed to react with oxygen to resupply the carbonate that reacted at the anode. For this reason, we must transfer CO_2 efficiently from the fuel to the air streams.

In a preliminary study [10] we have shown that potassium carbonate dispersed on fine alumina can sorb CO_2 faster than pure carbonate and can be regenerated thermally. The reaction was

$$CO_2 + H_2O + K_2CO_3 \cdot xH_2O \rightarrow 2KHCO_3 + xH_2O. \tag{2}$$

In this paper we present extensive new experimental data and a kinetic model for this reaction. New and old room temperature sorption data are summarized in Fig. 2.1. The improvement in rates of reaction at high CO_2 concentrations with disper sed carbonate was greater than anticipated [10], because new data and analysis have shown that the rate of sorption is proportional to the CO_2

concentration up to at least 20 percent CO_2. We also note that after a year of sorption and regeneration there was little change in appearance of the powder.

Rate data based on plate area as shown in Fig. 2.2 are useful for obtaining an estimate of the area needed for a given CO_2 duty with the sorbent packed exactly as done in this study. For example, the sorption area is several times smaller than the fuel cell area at 100 ma/cm².

In a practical device however, the sorbent may, for example, be formed into a sheet using some small amount of binder or even formed into pellets. Then we must know how to use the rate information determined in this study. One of the objects of this paper is to show that the rate for the carbonate-alumina mixture can be properly scaled using the initial weight of the carbonate. This turns out to be the correct scale factor, because all the data can be best correlated by a continuum model with no diffusional resistances. Thus, rates such as those shown in Fig. 2.1 are the most useful for design. From either Fig. 2.1 or Fig. 2.2 we see that cycle times must be short for a small device and we therefore suggest the use of a rotary mass exchanger with a sorption and a regeneration section.

APPARATUS AND PROCEDURE

APPARATUS

The sorbent or salt was held in a shallow depth pan over which mixtures of carbon dioxide and water could be passed. The pan and salt formed a part of a rectangular channel which has three functional sections: entrance, sorption, and exit sections. The channel was equipped with an inlet sampling system and outlet mixing chamber so that an inlet and outlet gas composition of mixture gas could be continuously measured. A schematic diagram of the apparatus is shown in Fig. 2.3. The sorption section was maintained at constant temperature. It could be heated by electric heaters or cooled by air or water flowing through flattened copper coils as required.

The overall length of the channel was 1.52 m with 0. 69 m of entrance region. The walls of the channel were made from type 304 stainless steel plates, 10.2 cm wide by 1.52m long and 0. 32 cm thick. The inside surface of these plates was polished to a No. 2B finish (i. e., dull, not quite mirrorlike polish). Spacer strips of the same material and length as the plates were held between the plates by 0. 64 cm bolts at staggered intervals of 10. 2 cm. The strips, 0. 32 cm thick and 1. 27 cm wide, were secured between the plates formed the flat rectangular channel with internal dimensions of 7. 62 cm by 0.32 cm. General Electric's "RTV 106" silicone rubber compound, capable of withstanding 315 °C, was used as a thin film gasket material to seal leaks between the plates and strips of the channel.

The entrance section was wrapped with several electric tape heaters to form a preheat region and an adiabatic region directly before the sorption section. All heated portions of the channel were wrapped with low conductivity insulation. The power supply for each heater was regulated through variacs.

In the sorption section, a shallow pan, 0. 16 cm deep by 7. 62 cm wide cm and 39. 69 cm long, was machined into a 0. 64 cm thick copper plate. This pan was filled with salt and then clamped to an opening in the channel. The copper plate fit into the channel so that the inside channel wall was flush with the surface of the salt, as shown in Fig. 2.4a. Also, to prevent the finely powdered salt from being blown out of the pan, a teflon-coated 145 mesh stainless steel screen was secured over the salt surface. The salt was exposed to a constant inlet gas mixture stream for the experimental runs. The carbon dioxide-nitrogen stream was saturated to 22 °C dew point. It was kept at constant temperature during the runs and regenerated by heating up to 204 °C with flat ceramic encased heaters surrounding the sorption section. Although regeneration took place at 82 °C at an appreciable rate, heating was continued to assure quantitative regeneration.

The exit section extended about 0 46 m beyond the sorption section. Tape heaters were used in this region to prevent water condensation inside the channel and to avoid severe temperature gradients along the channel. The transition from the rectangular channel to a 3. 81 cm diameter exhaust pipe was provided by a fabricated stainless steel baffled mixing chamber, and beyond the mixing chamber a valve was installed to maintain the pressure in the channel at 10 to 20 cm of water to prevent any leaks into the channel. A similarly fabricated transition piece was used at the entrance of the channel.

The various compositions of carbon dioxide and nitrogen were mixed and analyzed by Matheson Gas Products Co. The channel flow rate range was from 7.1 to 71.0 standard liters per minute. This was measured with rotameters calibrated against a bell prover-corrected wet-test meter and a "Laminar Flow Element" supplied and calibrated by the Meriam Company.

The concentration of carbon dioxide in the inlet and outlet gas streams was measured with an infrared analyzer manufactured by Mine Safety Appliances Company, Lira Model 300. The measuring ranges used were 0-0.5 and 0-2.0 mole percent CO_2 and the observed accuracy of the instrument was about of the full scale reading. This instrument was well suited to measure the concentration changes of carbon dioxide continuously. Its output was recorded on a Honeywell "Electronic 14" chart recorder. A direct and continuous measurement method in rate studies has obvious advantages over other techniques. Analyzing collected samples chromatographically or chemically, for instance, cannot generate large quantities of data as simply and quickly.

The moisture content of the gas streams was measured with a dew point hygrometer made by Cambridge Systems, Inc., Model 992. The hygrometer was also capable of measuring any changing moisture conditions. A Sargent recorder, Model SRG, was used to record the output.

Both the hygrometer and the infrared analyzer were placed as close as possible to the outlet stream from the sorption section: approximately 0.91 m. The 2.44 m length of sampling line was not significant since the inlet condition was not changing with time. The sampling system was made of hydrophobic materials: 0.64 cm diameter tubing and flow control valves of stainless steel and all packings and seals of tenon.

PREPARATION OF SORBENT

The salt used for this investigation was reagent grade anhydrous potassium carbonate supplied by J. T. Baker Chemical Co. A practically useful mixture of this salt with powdered alumina was chosen to be the sorbent after previous study with the pure salt. The mixture was 20 weight percent anhydrous potassium carbonate and 80 weight percent dried alumina. The alumina powder used was aluminum oxide "C" from DeGussa, Inc. Weighed portions of the potassium carbonate, which was granular like table salt, and the finely powdered alumina (average particle size about 20 milli-microns) were ground in a ball mill for about 7 hours. The ball mill was in a humidity-controlled room maintained at 12-15 percent relative humidity at 23 °C. Any weighing errors due to water and carbon dioxide pickup from the air were small. The copper support pan held about 40 grams of uncompacted mixture. To avoid a large loss of powder composition into the ball jar walls, 75 grams of mixture were ground. The walls were carefully scraped of powder and this was remixed with the bulk. The particle size distribution, surface area, and chemical composition were determined upon completion of all scheduled runs. Note that the same salt was used for one year of runs during which over 100 runs were made. The average size of a particle was $2\propto$ as shown in Fig. 2.5. The BET surface area was determined to be 59.5 m^2/gm.

EXPERIMENTAL PROCEDURE

The prepared salt mixture was carefully poured into its copper support pan and the screen mesh placed over its surface. The copper plate was then clamped into its channel opening and sealed with the silicone rubber compound. During the preparation and transportation of the salt it could pick up some carbon dioxide and water. Therefore, before the first run was begun, the salt was heated. During procedure and subsequent regenerations of the salt, dry nitrogen gas (−60 °C dew point) was passed through the channel and the-outlet concentration of carbon dioxide was continuously monitored with the infrared analyzer until the outlet concentration of carbon dioxide reached zero. The dry nitrogen flow rate was maintained at a constant low value of 5.95 standard liters per minute for all regenerations. This low flow rate produced measurable outlet concentrations of carbon dioxide in the "best" portion of the analyzer's range.

The first sorption run was not made until the salt and channel cooled to a constant temperature with dry nitrogen continually passing through the channel. The temperature was measured with thermocouples attached to the plate and channel sections. For the sorption process, the dry nitrogen was switched to wet nitrogen (22 °C dew point at 5.95 l/min) and allowed to flow over the salt for 35 minutes. Even though the mixture gas of carbon dioxide and nitrogen was saturated, the wet nitrogen made it certain that enough water was available. During the 35 minutes of pre-wetting, constant inlet conditions were obtained and recorded. After 35 minutes, the inlet mixture gas was switched into the channel by solenoid-operated valves. The infrared analyzer responded three seconds after the stream switching due to the holdup slug of nitrogen in the channel, and then about 1. 5 minutes after the switch, it tracked the slowly rising outlet concentration of carbon dioxide. Because of this, initial, sorption rates could only be estimated. The sorption process was halted when the outlet concentration approached approximately 98 percent of the inlet concentration, because of the analyzer's accuracy limitations. At the end of the run, the inlet mixture gas was switched to dry nitrogen gas and regeneration heating begun.

For runs with CO_2 inlet concentrations greater than 2 percent and for the study with pure salt, rates of sorption were obtained from differences in quantities of carbon dioxide liberated during regeneration. This procedure was necessary for the runs with high inlet carbon dioxide concentrations because there were negligibly small differences between the inlet and outlet concentrations during sorption even at the lowest flow rates possible in the apparatus with reasonable hold up. Hence the sorption process was allowed to continue for a certain interval of time, then the salt was regenerated. Each successive interval of time was increased. The amount of carbon dioxide sorbed in each time interval was calculated from the amount desorbed during regeneration.

DATA ANALYSIS

CALCULATION OF OVERALL RATES

Outlet concentration data from the Lira infrared analyzer were converted into rates of reaction which are called overall rates, since at low flow rates they are flow dependent.

An expression for an overall rate of sorption of CO_2 by K_2CO_3 in the apparatus can be obtained from an overall mass balance on the system containing the salt section, as shown in Fig. 2.4b where 2a equals 0.32 cm.

The overall rate of sorption is given by

$$r_{OV} = \frac{Q\rho}{60}(\omega_{in} - \omega_{out})/LW \tag{3}$$

where
Q (l/min), is the volumetric flow rate at STP,

ω (g CO_2/ g total), the mass fraction of CO_2,
ρ (g total/l)), the mass density of the total mixture,
L, W (cm), the length and width of the salt surface, equal to 39.69 and 7.62 cm, respectively.

The overall rate of sorption obtained from the CO_2 liberated during regeneration is

$$r_{OV} = \frac{1}{A_{surf}(\Delta t)} \int_0^\tau \rho Q \omega_{out} dt, \tag{4}$$

where
A_{surf} (cm^2), the plane surface area of the salt, $= LW$,

Δt (min), the time of the sorption run,

τ (min), the time of completed regeneration.

Rates obtained from regeneration runs are flow independent, since high flows were used during sorption.

INTEGRAL EQUATION ANALYSIS

At low CO_2 concentrations sorption proceeded for a sufficiently long time that we could obtain rates from outlet concentrations of CO_2 rather than from the more time- consuming series of regeneration runs. However, to handle such data we must correct for the diffusional resistance in the channel. Rates of sorption independent of diffusion in the gas phase can be obtained by an integral equation analysis already described in detail in our preliminary study [10] and previously [11] for catalytic combustion in a tube.

A two-dimensional mass balance for the sorption system is made, as shown in Fig. 2.4b. The total density is constant, since the temperature is maintained constant and the system is dilute with respect to water and carbon dioxide up to Due to the diluteness of the system, a constant effective diffusivity is used. Fully developed laminar flow is achieved by means of a long entrance section. Then the mass balance on CO_2. results in the partial differential equation given as

$$\frac{3}{2}U\left[1-(\frac{y_A}{a})^2\right]\frac{\partial \omega}{\partial x_A} = D\frac{\partial^2 \omega}{\partial y_A^2},$$
(5)

with boundary conditions

$$\omega(0,y_A) = \omega_{in}, \text{ constant, } -a < y_A < a,$$
(6a)

$$\frac{\partial \omega}{\partial y_A}(x_A,a) = 0,$$
(6b)

$$\rho D\frac{\partial \omega}{\partial y_A}(x_A,-a) = \text{(rate of sorption)}.$$
(6c)

Integration- of Eqs. (5), (6a), (6b) and (6c) yields the expression for the flow-independent sorption rate as a function of the contact time, $R(x)$:

$$\frac{4}{3}\frac{dC_m}{dx} = -R(x) = -\left\{\frac{a\cdot(rate)}{\rho D\omega_{in}}\right\}. \tag{7}$$

The mixing cup concentration, C_m was fitted to a polynomial in x and the wall concentration at a given x was found from the integral representation of the boundary value problem.

EXPERIMENTAL RATES

Rates of sorption for essentially zero contact time (see Fig. 2.6) obtained from the integral equation analysis had the smallest variance. Therefore, we use only these rates in further discussion of low CO_2 data.

In Fig. 2.6 we see how the flow-independent rate of sorption varies with sorption time for different CO_2 compositions. The most interesting behavior is obtained by replotting these rates versus CO_2 concentration. In Fig. 2.7 a straight line could be drawn through the estimated initial data points. The reaction is therefore first order with respect to CO_2. The zero-time data in Fig. 2.7 were obtained by extrapolating the initially exponentially decreasing rate with time, as shown in Fig. 2.6. Such an extrapolation is safe, since many gas-solid reactions exhibit such an exponential decay and because such an initial drop can be explained by a model which considers plugging of pores due to accumulation of the product [12]. The rate constant at zero time is 0.434 cm/ s; initially the dimensionless group, $ka / D = 0.5$ showing that diffusion in the channel should be corrected for [13].

Now consider the concentration gradient across the thickness of the sorbent. For a first-order reaction it is best characterized by the Thiele modulus [14, 15]. For zero-sorption time the Thiele modulus based on the slab of sorbent held in the pan is 0.6. It gives an effectiveness factor of 0.93 [14]. This means that the maximum concentration. gradient from the top particle in the pan to the bottom particle is seven percent. The layer of the sorbent was sufficiently thin not to require a correction for this effect, even at zero time where the error is largest.

Fig. 2.7 also shows us that as time of sorption proceeds, the rate changes from a first-order behavior to one that is nearly independent of concentration. Such behavior is not totally unexpected, although it does not appear to have been dealt with in the literature explicitly. Consider the unreacted-core shrinking model for a spherical particle as described, for example, in Levenspiel's book [16] For chemical reaction control, the fraction of carbonate unreacted, X_A, is related to concentration of CO_2, C_{in}, by

$$(1 - X_A^{\frac{1}{3}}) = C_{in}(\frac{t}{\tau_{cr}}), \tag{8}$$

where $\tau_{cr} = \dfrac{\rho_B R_B}{bk_s}$ and is unknown in our system and where t is sorption time. The rate of reaction that we observe is proportional to

$\dfrac{dX_A}{dt}$ which is given by

$$-\frac{dX_A}{dt} = 3[1 - C_{in}(\frac{t}{\tau_{cr}})]^2(\frac{C_{in}}{\tau_{cr}}). \tag{9}$$

After a certain time of sorption, this function will clearly have a maximum with concentration, C_{in}. Its behavior is displayed in Fig. 2.8 where $\bar{\tau} = {t}/{\tau_{cr}}$. Qualitatively it is similar to the measured rates. Thus, the observed behavior could in part be due to the decreased surface area for reaction. Quantitative comparison is best done by comparing the fraction reacted versus time for different concentrations and will be discussed later.

Data obtained from regeneration runs at 5, 10, and 20 percent CO_2 confirmed the first-order behavior at zero time, as seen in Fig.

2.9. The rate constant based on the plate area, as already mentioned, is 0.043 ± 0.012 cm/s.

The fraction of carbonate reacted was calculated for various compositions by numerically integrating the rates of reaction as a function of time, as displayed in Fig. 2.10. As expected, we see that at higher concentrations, the fraction converted is higher for the same sorption time. The maximum observed conversion was about 70 percent. The same conversion was observed by measuring a depression in CO_2 pressure when the sorbent was suddenly introduced into a flask containing CO_2. This phenomenon is attributed to pore closing [12].

To determine the effect of humidity, the four possible combinations of runs were made: 1) the usual presaturation with wet CO_2 inlet gas, 2) no presaturation but wet CO_2 gas, 3) pre saturation but bone dry CO_2 gas, 4) no presaturation and bone dry gas. At low flow rates we see from Fig. 2.11 that the first three cases yield essentially the same rates. In case 4 there is no reactant present. The negligibly small rate obtained represents physical adsorption of CO_2 on the high surface area s or bent. Runs W7 and W8 are at a higher flow and should strictly speaking, be compared with each other only and with a normal run at the same flow. We see that at higher times, these high flow runs diverge a little more than the others. After some time, with dry inlet gases, much of the water initially present is used up and the rate must drop due to a deficiency in water in parts of the salt. Thus although water content and humidity does not affect the initial rates of sorption markedly, it is best to operate with an excess of water.

The temperature of the sorbent was varied from 24 °C to 150 °C maintaining the inlet CO_2 concentration constant at one mole percent CO_2 and the flow rate at a sufficiently high value for the effect of convective diffusion to be small. The results are shown in Fig. 2.12. Rates at zero time allowing for scatter of the data, were essentially independent of temperature from 24 to about 80 °C. At times greater than two minutes, they decreased with temperature. The decomposition pressure of potassium bicarbonate at 80 °C shows that we should not expect much sorption of CO_2 from a one percent mixture. However, we see appreciable sorption all the way to 150 °C. This indicates an interaction between potassium carbonate and alumina which results in a lower CO_2 tension. Such an interaction was also observed for sorption of water on lithium chloride impregnated asbestos [17]. As a result of this increased sorption at high temperatures, regeneration had to be carried out at above 200 °C to obtain material balances between sorption and subsequent regeneration of CO_2.

CONVENTIONAL MODELS

UNREACTED SHRINKING CORE MODELS

The striking similarity between Figs. 7 and 8, both showing a decrease in the reaction order with the time of reaction, demands a quantitative test of the data to the unreacted-shrinking core model. The first indication of work in connection with this model known to the authors appears in a 1939 German book edited by Jacob and Eucken [18] who give earlier literature references. More recently, this model has been described in books by Levenspiel[16] and Smith [19]. An article showing the applicability of this model to large ≈ 1.7 cm particles is by Gokarn and Doraiswamy [20]. In 1965, White and Carberry cited a criterion credited to R. L. Gorring for the applicability of the shell progressive model which states that the Thiele modulus must be greater than 200 for the model to hold [21]. In 1970 Calvelo and Cunningham refined this criterion and stated that the shrinking core model will be satisfactory from a rigorous point of view only when the solid is nonporous [22]. Two years earlier Ishida and Wen also noted the need for a new model to handle the case of porous solids [23].

We tested the applicability of the models with 0. 5 to 2 percent CO_2 data, as discussed by Wen [24] The data were plotted according to the relations predicted by the model between the fraction of solid reactant unconverted, the time of reaction, and the inlet gas concentration. Both rate controlling mechanisms were considered;

that is, ash diffusion and chemical reaction control. No satisfactory fit was achieved as is seen in Fig. 2.13. A successful fit should converge the data onto one straight line in Fig. 2.13 [24]. We also applied the shrinking core models to our particle distribution. No correlation was obtained. Flat plate geometry also gives no agreement with the data, as already discussed in our preliminary study [10].

We conclude that the unreacted-shrinking core models cannot represent the data of this study. This conclusion is supported by the fact that our particles are small and porous. We already stated that the largest possible Thiele modulus, based on sorbent thickness is 0.6. The Thiele modulus based on the particle diameter is much smaller. Thus, we are nowhere near the condition for the applicability of the shrinking core models.

EQUILIBRIUM MODELS

Sorption data are frequently analyzed using models that assume the rates of reaction to be so fast that equilibrium exists at every point in the particle and that the uptake of the gas is controlled by diffusion into the particles. A study by Marcussen of water adsorption by 2 mm particles of porous alumina is an example of where such a model is applicable [25]. His equilibrium model is applicable because the vapor pressure of water is appreciable and the particles are large. In our case the decomposition pressure of the potassium bicarbonate is zero with respect to the gas concentrations at and near room temperature.

Nevertheless, we tried to apply such models to our data. Disregarding the observed pore closing, we show the expected final or pseudo-equilibrium conversion in Fig. 2.14 where the points were obtained by extrapolating the rate data to infinite time as done by Marcussen [25]. Note that for 5, 1 0 and 20% CO_2 nearly complete conversion is predicted due to the method of extrapolation which assumes that the exponential relation continues to hold true. The half to two-percent CO_2 data in Fig. 2.14 can be approximated by a straight line, that is, we approximate it by a linear equilibrium curve. Then the resulting diffusion equation has a well-known analytical solution. It shows that the rate of sorption is proportional to the concentration for all times. This is in marked disagreement with our observation, as depicted in Fig. 2.7. Only at zero time is the rate proportional to the CO_2 concentration. This fact, also precludes the applicability of a bidisperse pore structure model proposed by Ruckenstein, Vaidyanathan, and Youngquist [27]. Their model predicts a sorption rate that is linear in CO_2 concentration for all times of sorption, no matter how much of the sorbent is consumed.

WITH VARIABLE PORE STRUCTUREi

In 1957 Peterson presented a sophisticated extension of Thiele's classical analysis to the case when the pore structure changes with reaction [28]. He treated the single-pore model whose pore radius increases linearly with time at a constant gas concentration and a cylindrical pellet model with random pore intersections. To compare our data with Peterson's models, we recall that our Thiele modulus, even when based on sorbent layer thickness, is small. We therefore compare his predictions for zero Thiele modulus to our data. Peterson's models do not give a rate of reaction that decreases exponentially with time. Therefore, his models do not apply to our situation.

In 1970 Calvelo and Cunningham continued Peter son's analysis [29]. Their solution for large Thiele modulus is of no interest in this study. Their limiting case of surface area varying with the 2/3 power of solid concentration again gives a time variation of rate inconsistent with our data. The rate of consumption of K_2CO_3 is clearly not proportional to the 2/3 power of concentration. In the next section we see that it is directly proportional to it, as is. the case for many other fluid-consumable porous solid reactions [12].

CONTINUUM MODEL

Experimentally observed exponential variation of rates with time and incomplete conversion can be explained by a model proposed by Gidaspow [12]. The model is called a continuum model, because reaction is as assumed to take place homogeneously throughout a volume element without consideration of any specific pore structure. A material balance for a solid S, in this case K_2CO_3, gave the differential equation

$$\frac{d}{dt}(V\varepsilon_s\rho_s) = -r_v\varepsilon_sV .$$ (10)

For a constant volume, V, the conventional solid reactant concentration, C_s, is related to the volume fraction of S, ε_s, through the true density of K_2CO_3 as

$$C_s = \rho_s\varepsilon_s .$$ (11)

Then in more conventional terms Eq. (10) can be written as

$$\frac{dC_s}{dt} = -r_wC_s ,$$ (12)

where $r_w = \dfrac{r_v}{\rho_s}$.

The rate that we measured, R, in terms of grams of K_2CO_3 converted per gram of K_2CO_3 initially present per unit time becomes

$$R = r_we^{-r_wt} .$$ (13)

This is the expression for the rate when the solid reactant is consumed by a single reaction and is cornpletely diffusionally accessible. Figure 3 in the paper by Gidaspow I shows that an exponential expression of the form of Eq. (13) holds even for high Thiele moduli but with rates at zero time multiplied by an effectiveness factor. We have

$$R = \eta r_we^{-r_wt} ,$$ (14)

where η is the conventional effectiveness factor used in catalytic reactions. Note that the slope in the plot of $\ln R$ versus t gives the rate unaffected by diffusion, while the intercept yields a rate masked by diffusion. Slopes and intercepts for the data for the K_2CO_3-alumina sorbent determined in the manner just described are shown in columns two and three of Table 2.I. The rates obtained from both the slopes and the intercepts are the same for 5, 10 and 20% CO_2 and not too different for 2% CO_2. This means that the effectiveness factor for our reagent is unity.

However, due to a consistent difference at low concentrations a correction to the basic mechanism becomes necessary. We see this clearly in Fig. 2.15 when we plot the rate values from the slope versus CO_2 concentration. While the initial rates went through zero at zero concentration, these rates have a small positive value at zero CO_2 concentration. A negative value could have indicated an equilibrium hindrance. A positive value indicates that the solid reactant is consumed or becomes inaccessible by some other reaction than one that depends directly upon CO_2 concentration. For the solid reactant consumed by two reactions the material balance is given by

$$\frac{d}{dt}(V\varepsilon_s \rho_s) = -(r_{v1} + r_{v2})\varepsilon_s V. \tag{15}$$

If the second reaction is competitive and does not consume CO_2, the rate that we measure becomes

$$R = r_{w1} \exp[-(r_{w1} + r_{w2})t], \tag{16}$$

where r_{w1} is proportional to CO_2 concentration and r_{w2} is a constant. The slow competitive reaction may be formation of a solution which blocks the remaining solid.

Data fitted to the form of Equation (15) produced the following equation for the alumina- K_2CO_3 sorbent:

$$R = 3.5x_{CO_2} \exp[-(3.5x_{CO_2} + 2.32)t], \tag{17}$$

where x_{CO_2} is mole percent CO_2, t is time in hours, and R is expressed in terms of grams of K_2CO_3 converted, based on CO_2 sorbed, per gram of K_2CO_3 initially present per hour. The standard deviations for 3.5 and 2.32 are 0.084 and 0.73, respectively. Fig. 2.16 gives a comparison of this fit to the data. Deviations that occur at higher times or conversion, at low CO_2 concentrations, are due to pore closing expected from the modeling studies [12]. Since these deviations are srnall — the logarithmic plot in Fig. 2.16 exaggerates them — and since we did not determine the void fraction in the 2 μ particles while the experimental phase was in progress, a quantitative comparison is not given. The effectiveness factors corrected for the competitive reaction are shown to be close to unity in Table 2.I. These are, of course, as already explained, meaningful only until the pore closing makes itself felt. This occurs near the pore closing condition [12]. Integration of Eq. (16) disregarding the observed incomplete conversion, gives the equation represented in Fig. 2.14.

PRESSED SHEET OF K_2CO_3

PREPARATION OF PURE SALT

This reagent was prepared as follows: 58 grams of reagent grade, granular anhydrous potassium carbonate were ground in a mortar to a fine powder in a low humidity control room. This was poured into the channel support plate and pressed in a hydraulic press with one hundred and fifty tons of force. The pressed carbonate had a measured average porosity of 30%, with a mean pore diameter of 8 microns. Eighty percent of the porosity was due to pores of $0.1 \approx 10$ microns diameter.

DATA AND ANALYSIS

Fig. 2.1 and Fig. 2.2 show the reaction data for the pure salt. Five to 100% CO_2 data were obtained by the regeneration method. Lower concentration data were calculated from outlet concentrations and are somewhat affected by flow rate because insufficient number of runs were made to make an integral equation analysis to determine a good correction.

Table 2.Il presents rates and effectiveness factors calculated according to Eq. (14). We see that the effectiveness factors are of the order of 0.1 in a marked contrast to the complete effectiveness achieved with the alumina- K_2CO_3 sorbent. Further we see a consistent increase of effectiveness with concentration of the gas. This is in agreement with the theory presented by Gidaspow [12]. Effectiveness is better at higher concentrations, because as CO_2 reacts, there is a reduction in volume which causes the gas to be sucked in. For a dilute system an effectiveness factor of 0.1 gives a Thiele modulus of ten for a flat plate. Using the rate constant for the alumina- K_2CO_3 sorbent of 5.4 s^{-1}, the effective diffusion coefficient becomes equal to 1.4 x 10^{-3} cm/s. Diffusion coefficients of this order of magnitude are observed in pressed powders.

ACKNOWLEDGEMENT

This study was supported by a grant from the Pratt and Whitney Division of United Aircraft Corporation and by the Institute of Gas Technology Basic Research Program. The initial experimental phase of this study was done by K. Soda and L. K. Leung. The authors would also like to thank B. S. Baker for a useful discussion of various aspects of this problem.

NOMENCLATURE

a = one-half the distance between the sorbing and non- sorbing wall for channel flow, 0.16 cm

A_{surf} = plane surface area of salt in channel, LW

b = stoichiometric coefficient ratio in unreacted-core shrinking model, moles of solid reactant/ mole of gaseous reactant

C = dimensionless concentration, $(\omega - \omega_{eq})/(\omega_{in} - \omega_{eq})$

C_{in} = concentration of CO_2 in inlet gas stream

C_m = dimensionless mixing cup concentration, defined by Eq. (7)

C_S = conventional solid concentration of S

D = molecular diffusivity, cm²/s

D_{ash} = effective diffusivity of gas through ash in unreacted-core shrinking model, cm²/s

k = rate constant, s⁻¹

---

k_s = rate constant for solid reaction in unreacted-core shrinking model, chemical reaction control case, s^{-1}

L = length of sorption wall, 39. 69 cm

Q = volumetric flow rate at STP, 21 °C and 1 atm, 1pm

r = rate of reaction

r_{OV} = overall rate of reaction, $(gCO_2 / m^2 - \sec)(K_2CO_3 - hr)$

r_V = mass rate of consumption of solid S per unit volume of S, (gS/cm^3 S-s)

r_{V1}, r_{V2} = mass rate of consumption of solid S per unit volume of S by primary reaction for subscript v1, and by competitive reaction for subscript v2, (gS/cm^3 S-s)

r_W = intrinsic mass rate of consumption of S, s^{-1}, ρ_S / r_V

r_{W1}, r_{W2} – intrinsic mass rate of consumption of S by primary reaction for subscript w1, ρ_S/r_{V1}, and by competitive reaction for subscript w2, ρ_S/r_{V2}, s^{-1}

R = dimensionless reaction rate $\dfrac{4}{3}\dfrac{dC_m}{dx}$, also measured rate of reaction, (gS/gS-s)

R_P = radius of spherical particle in unreacted-core shrinking model

Re = Reynolds number, $(4aU\rho / \mu)$

S = solid reactant, K_2CO_3

Sc = Schmidt number, $(\mu / \rho D)$

t = time

t^* = interval time for numerical integration of rate data, min

U = mass average velocity, $(Q/12aW)$, m/s

V = bulk volume of solid, cm^3

Var = variance

W = width of sorption wall, 7.62 cm

$W_\circ$ = final weight of potassium carbonate converted, gK_2CO_3

W_{max} = maximum theoretical weight of potassium carbonate that can react, gK_2CO_3

x = dimensionless special coordinate parallel to flow (dimensionless contact time), $(8x_A/3aReSc)$; also unknown stoichiometric coefficient in Eq. (1)

x_A = special coordinate parallel to flow direction, cm

x_{CO_2} = mole percent CO_2

X_A = fraction of carbonate unreacted

X_B = fraction of carbonate converted, $(1 - X_A)$

y = dimensionless special coordinate perpendicular to flow direction, (y_A / a)

y_A = special coordinate perpendicular to flow direction, origin at centerline of channel's width, cm

GREEK LETTERS

η = conventional effectiveness factor used in catalytic reactions

ρ = mass density of total mixture, g/l

ρ_B = molar density of solid reactant in particle in unreacted core-shrinking model, moles solid/cm^3

ρ_S = void free density of solid S, (gS/cm^3 S)

τ = time of completed regeneration, min

τ_{ad} = constant related to time for completed conversion in ash-diffusion control case of unreacted-core shrinking model, $(\rho_B R_p^2 / 6bD_{ash})$

τ_{cr} – constant related to time for completed conversion in chemical reaction control case of unreacted-core shrinking model, $(\rho_B R_p / bk_s)$

$\bar{\tau}$ = time related to constant obtained from chemical reaction control case of unreacted-core shrinking model, $(t / \tau_{cr}), (bk_s t / \rho_B R_p)$

ω = weight fraction

ω_{eq} = equilibrium weight fraction

ω_{in} = inlet weight fraction

ω_{out} = outlet weight fraction

REFERENCES

1. Sherwood, T. K. and Pigford, R. L., "Absorption and Extraction", McGraw-Hill, New York (1952).
2. Astarita, G., "Mass Transfer with Chemical Reaction", American Elsevier, New York (1967).
3. Danckwerts, P. V., "Gas-Liquid Reactions", McGraw-Hill, New York (1970).
4. Weber, O. W., Miller, I. F., and Gregor, H. P., "The Absorption of Carbon Dioxide by Weak Base Ion Exchange Resins," AIChE J., 16, 609-19 July (1970).
5. Schecter, W. H., "Porous Anhydrous Lithium Hydroxide Granules", U. S. Patent No. 2,629,652, February (1953).
6. Williams, D. D. and Miller, R. R., "Effect of Water Vapor on the LiOH-CO_2 Reaction", I & EC Fundamentals, 9, 454-7 August (1970).
7. Colombo, G. V. and Mills, E. S., "Regenerative Separation of Carbon Dioxide via Metallic Oxides", Chem. Eng. Prog. Syrnp. Series No. 63, 62, 89-94 (1966).
8. Gluckert, A. J., Nuccio, P. P., and Zeff, J. D., "GAT-O-SORB – A Regenerable Sorbent for Carbon Dioxide Control", Society of Automotive Engineers, Aeronautic and Space Engineering and Manufacturing Meeting, Los Angeles, CA., October 2-6, 1967.
9. Liebhafsky, H. A. and Cairns, E. J., "Fuel Cells and Fuel Batteries. A Guide to Their Research and Development", Wiley, New York (1968).
10. Gidaspow, D. and Onischak, M., "Regenerative Sorption of CO_2", AIChE Symp. Ser., 68, No. 120, p 11.6-23 (1972).
11. Gidaspow, D., "Green's Functions for the Graetz Problem and Interfacial Concentrations", AIChE J., 17, 19-24 January (1971).
12. Gidaspow, Dimitri, "A Fluid-Porous Solid Reaction Model with Structural Changes", Proceedings of the 7th Intersociety

Energy Conversion Engineering Conference. Sept. 25-29 (1972).

13. Solbrig, C. W. and Gidaspow, D., "Convective Diffusion in a Parallel Plate Duct with One Catalytic Wall-Laminar Flow-First Order Reaction, Part I – Analytical", Can. J. Chem. Eng., 45, 35-40, February (1967).

14. Thiele, E. W., "Relation Between Catalytic Activity and Size of Particle", I & EC., 31, No. 7, 916-20, July (1939).

15. Satterfield, C. N. and Sherwood, T. K., "The Role of Diffusion in Catalysis", Addison- Wesley, Reading, Mass (1963).

16. Levenspiel, O., "Chemical Reaction Engineering", Wiley, New York (1962).

17. Rush, W. F. and Macriss, R. A., "Munters Environmental Control System", Appliance Engineer, 3, No. 3, 23-8 (1969).

18. "Der Chemie-lngenieur", Vol. Ill, edited by A. Eucken and M. Jakob, Leipzig (1939), Photo-Lithoprint Reproduction, Edward Bros, Ann Arbor, Mich. (1943).

19. Smith, J. M., "Chemical Engineering Kinetics", McGraw-Hill, New York (1970).

20. Gokarn, A. N. and Doraiswamy, L. K., "A Model for Solid-Gas Reactions", Chem. Eng. Sci., 26, 1521-33 (1971).

21. White, D. E. and Car berry, J. J., "Kinetics of Gas-Solid Non-Catalytic Reaction", Can. J. Chem. Eng., 43, 334-7 December (1965).

22. Calvelo, A. and Cunningham, R. E., "Criterion of Applicability of the Moving Boundary Model", J. Catal., 17, 143-150 (1970).

23. Ishida, M. and Wen, C. Y., "Comparison of Kinetic and Diffusional Models for Solid-Gas Reactions", AIChE J., 14, No. 2, 31 1-17, March (1968).

24. Wen, C. Y., "Noncatalytic Heterogeneous Solid Fluid Reaction Models", I & E C, 60, No. 9, 34-54, September (1968).

25. Marcussen, L., "The Kinetics of Water Adsorption on Porous Alumina", Chem. Eng. Sci., 25, 1487-99 (1970).

26. Crank, J., "The Mathematics of Diffusion", Oxford Univ. Press, London (1956).

27. Ruckenstein, E., Vaidyanathan, A. S., and Youngquist, G. R., "Sorption by Solids with Bidisperse Pore Structures", <u>Chem. Eng. Sci.</u>, <u>26</u>, 1305-18 (1971).
28. Petersen, E. E., "Reaction of Porous Solids", <u>AIChE J.</u>, <u>3</u>, No. 4, 443-48, December (1957).
29. Cavello, A. and Cunningham, R. E., "Kinetics of Gas-Solid Reactions, Influence of Surface Area and Effective Diffusivity Profiles", <u>J. Catal.</u>, <u>17</u>, 1-9 (1970).
30. Weisz, P. B., "Diffusivity of Porous Particles, I. Measurements and Significance for Internal Reaction Velocities", <u>Z. Phys. Chem. Neue Folge</u>, <u>11</u>, 1-15 (1957).

Table 2.I Rates and Effectiveness Factors for K_2CO_3-Alumina Sorbent

Inlet CO_2 Conc (mole %)	Intercept Value of Rate $(g\,K_2CO_3/g\,K_2CO_3\text{-hr})$	Initial Slope Value of Rate $(g\,K_2CO_3/g\,K_2CO_3\text{-hr})$	Corrected Slope Value by 2.32 hr^{-1}	Effectiveness $\eta =$ (Intercept Value/ Corrected Slope Value
20	70.6	72.8	70.5	1.0
10	34.5	37.2	34.9	0.989
5	15.1	16.9	14.6	1.03
2	7.46	9.5	7.18	1.04
1.5	4.86	8.6	6.28	0.774
1	2.73	6.7	4.38	0.623
0.5	1.92	4.3	1.98	0.970

Table 2.II Rates and Effectiveness Fctors for a Sheet of Pressed Pure K_2CO_3

Mole % CO_2	Rate $(g\,K_2CO_3/g\,K_2CO_3 - hr)$ from Intercept	from Slope	Effectiveness factor, $\eta = \dfrac{intercept}{slope}$
100	1.142	6.65	0.172
30	1.176	7.87	0.149
15	0.894	6.81	0.131
5	0.257	4.62	0.056
*0.92	0.176	5.47	0.032
*0.47	0.151	4.53	0.033
*0.12	0.060	2.36	0.025

* Uncorrected for convective diffusion

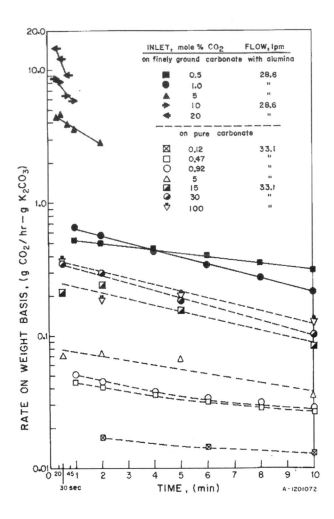

Fig. 2.1. Improvement in the rate of sorption of CO_2

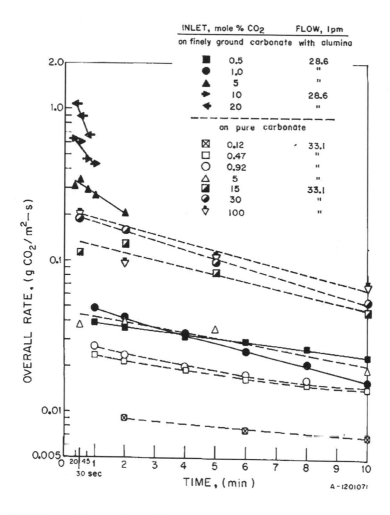

Fig. 2.2. Rate of sorption of CO_2 at 24 °C on a plate area basis

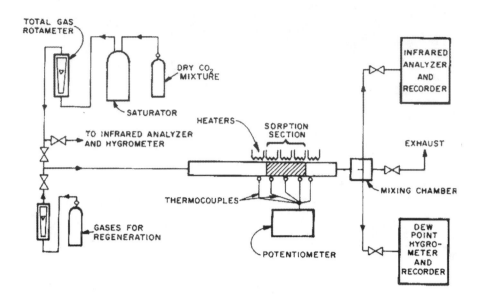

Fig. 2.3. Schematic diagram of apparatus

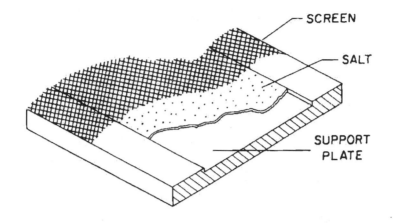

Fig. 2.4a Salt support section

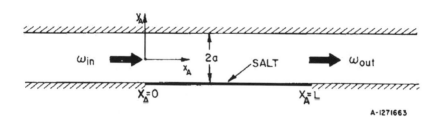

Fig 2.4b. Sorption section geometry

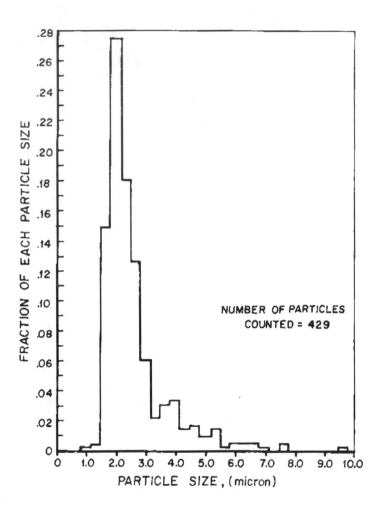

Fig. 2.5. Particle size distribution for alumina–K_2CO_3 sorbent

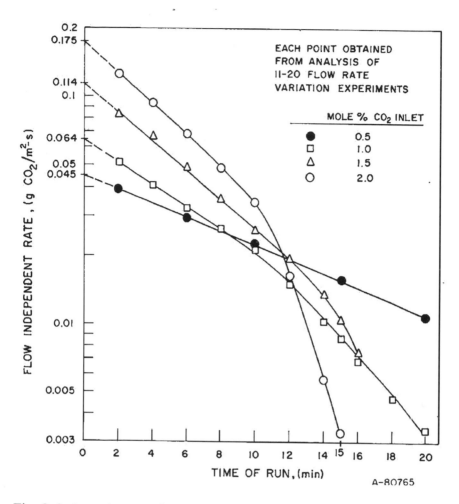

Fig. 2.6. Actual rates of sorption of CO_2 at 24 °C

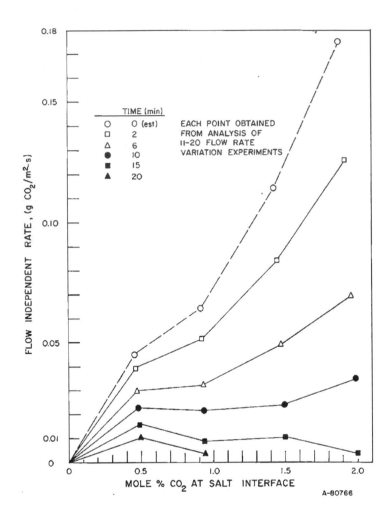

Fig. 2.7. Effect of CO_2 concentration on rates of sorption at 24 °C

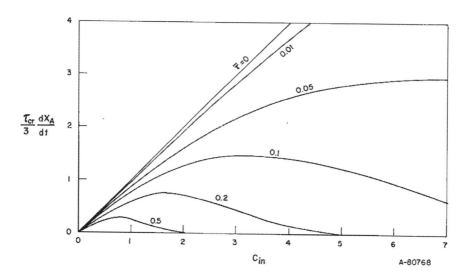

Fig. 2.8. Rate behavior as a function of concentration

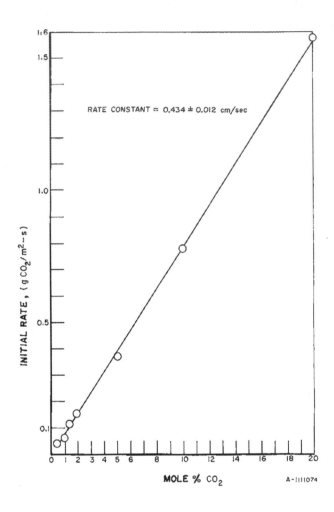

Fig. 2.9. First order behavior with respect to CO_2 extrapolated to zero time

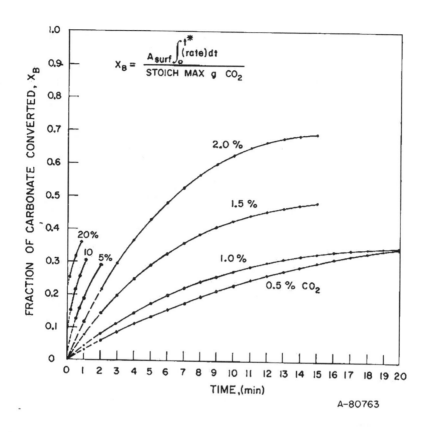

$$X_B = \frac{A_{surf} \int_o^{t^*} (rate)dt}{STOICH\ MAX\ g\ CO_2}$$

Fig. 2.10. Salt utilization based on K_2CO_3 in mixture

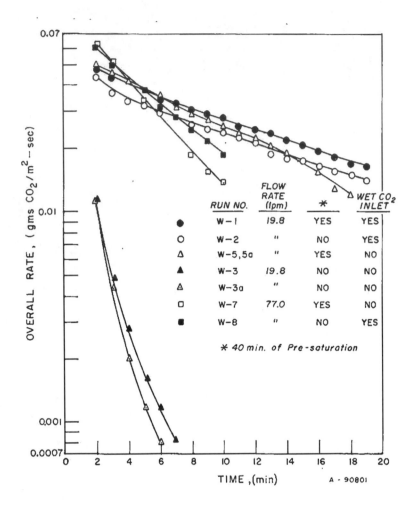

Fig. 2.11. Effect of humidity on rate of sorption

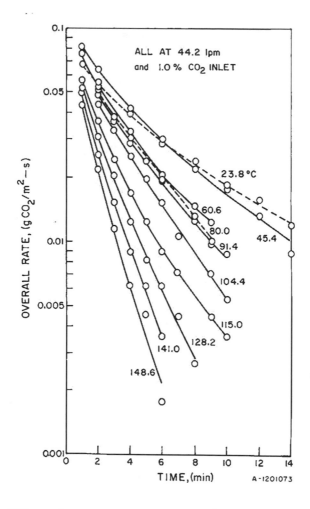

Fig. 2.12. Effect of temperature on rates of sorption

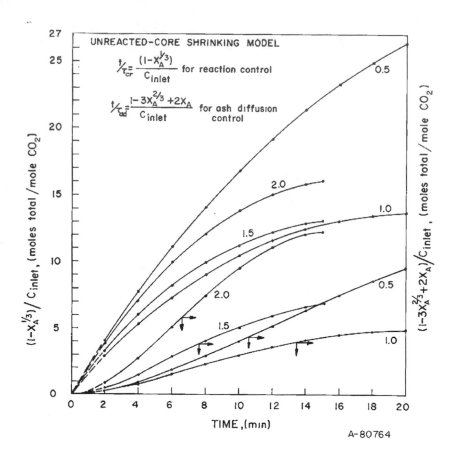

Fig. 2.13. Test of unreacted–core shrinking model

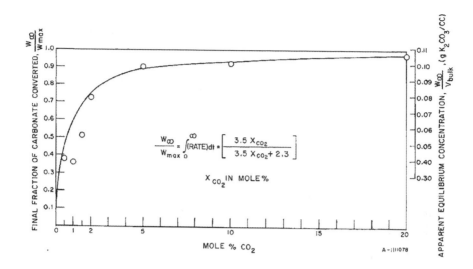

Fig. 2.14. Expected conversion with no pore closing

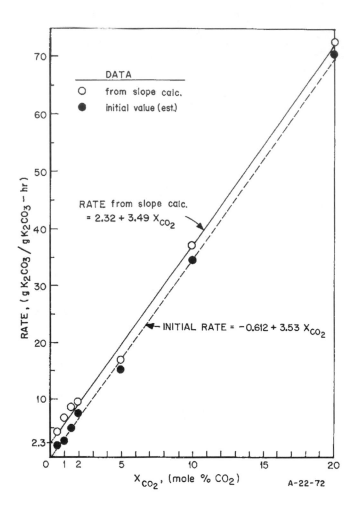

Fig. 2.15. Values of rate from slope and intercept of data

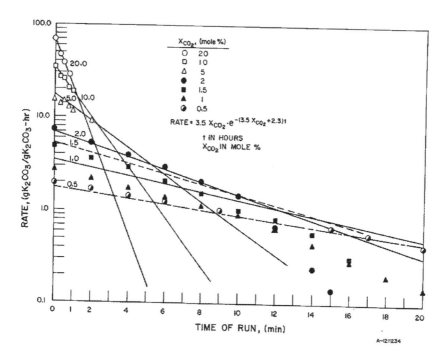

Fig. 2.16. Comparison of data with a fully-accessible continuum model

3

Silicon Deposition Reactor Using High Voltage Heating

ABSTRACT

This chapter deals with the preparation of high purity silicon by thermal decomposition of trichlorosilane, with its reaction with hydrogen, as in the Siemens process, and with the production of silicon from silane in fluidized bed reactors. Such fluidized bed reactors under active development are all heated by external heating. This requires the wall temperature to be higher than the decomposition temperature of the reactants. The high wall temperature causes the reactants to decompose at the wall, possibly producing a clinker that will cause reactor shut-down. When wall materials other than quartz, such as stainless steel, are used, the silicon gets contaminated, defeating the whole purification process. An alternative to stainless steel is the construction of the deposition reactor out of a high thermal conductivity alumina. Such a construction material was used by Gidaspow and Ellington [1] for combustion of hydrogen at high temperatures.

This chapter is based on the observation that the electrical conductivity of silicon particles in a fluidized bed is many orders of magnitude larger than the gas electrical conductivity. Hence with electrodes placed into fluidized beds, the particles will be heated to a higher temperature than the gases, causing the trichlorosilane to decompose on the particles rather than in the gas phase. Decomposition in the gas phase is known to cause formation of undesirable fines. In this method of heating, the reactor wall will be kept cold enough to prevent contamination of the product.

In view of the reasonably high resistance of the silicon particles in fluidized beds, the voltages to be applied are of the order of kilovolts, with currents in the range of millivolts. The size of the reactor and the flow rates dictate the actual values.

INTRODUCTION

The majority of polysilicon is produced by the Siemens hot bar method using purified silane or trichlorosilane as the source of silicon (Wooditsch and Koch [2]; Ege, et al. [3]). The fluidized bed reactors offer considerably higher production rates at a smaller energy consumption leading to expected order of magnitude lower costs for solar collectors. Hsu, et al. [4] have described the production of polysilicon from silane in a 15 cm diameter fluidized bed reactor. Their reactors, like the commercial reactors being built, are externally heated. Poong and Yongmok [5] have proposed a microwave internal heating method. However, they have provided too few details about their microwave system to properly evaluate their concept. It seems unlikely that their heating method can be easily applied to large fluidized beds. In contrast, the proposed technique simply involves inserting electrodes, made of or coated with silicon, into the fluidized beds, connected to a high voltage supply of alternating or direct current. The voltage needed depends on the size of the reactor given by a simple expression in terms of bed resistance and required power.

MEASUREMENT OF ELECTRICAL RESISTENCE OF FLUIDIZED BED OF SILICON PARTICLES

Resistance measurements were made in the IIT fluidized bed set-up shown in the attached figure. The set-up was similar to that used by Kashyap, et al. [6] for studying the effect of electric field on the flow of nanoparticles, with the bed rebuilt by Tiyapiboonchaiya et al. [7] for measuring the surface charge and fluidization of polypropylene particles. The bed dimensions are as follows: 1.0 inches wide × 2.75 inches between electrodes. The bed was filled with 350.3g of silicon particles (30% 600 microns and below, rest larger) to a height of 2.75inches.

The packed bed resistance was obtained by measuring the current and voltage upon connecting the copper electrodes to a positive and a negative power supplies No reliable resistance could be obtained by the use of conventional resistance measuring instruments, probably due to oxide film formation on the silicon particles.

Voltage, kV Current, mA Resistance, kΩ

6.9 17.7 390

4.0 11.3 380

2.56 4.5 568

1.23 1 1230

The nonlinear resistance in the table above is consistent with the lower silicon thin film resistance measured by Kim, et al. [8]. With a flow of air at a velocity of about one meter per second, normal bubbling fluidization is observed, as shown in Gidaspow and Jiradilok's [9] computer model.

Upon application of the electric field of 12 kvolts, the bed freezes quickly. An application of 6.5 kvolts gives a steady current of 19.7mA. The resistance is 329 kohms, somewhat lower than that for a packed bed, shown in the table above. The lower fluidized bed resistance is due to particle rearrangement, to minimize the dissipation of energy, as given by Prigogins's minimum entropy production principle.

Particle attraction to the electrodes is visible. Upon application of the electric field there was a rise of particle temperature to 90 °C in a few minutes, measured by a thermometer put into the bed. The large effect of the electric field on the fluidization of particles should allow one to control the flow and perhaps to separate the fines.

The fluidization with the application of the electric field is different from that without the applied field. In place of nearly spherical bubbles, there are thin slugs moving up the bed. Closer to normal behavior is obtained by increasing the flow rate. With a high flow rate the current drops to a small value, increasing the electrical resistance significantly. The bed resistivity, R_{sp} (kohms·cm) for 400 kohms is obtained from the standard formula: 400 kohms × distance between electrodes / cross sectional area for current flow = 1396 kohms·cm.

The pure silicon resistivity is about 83 kohms·cm for a silicon bar. Since the packed bed is only 50% silicon, the bed resistivity is only 8 times that of pure silicon. The high resistivity is due to poor particle contact and due to an oxide file formation on the particles.

ELECTRIC POWER DESIGN

The relatively high silicon fluidized bed resistance will require a high voltage supply to heat the silicon particles. The required voltage, V, can be easily computed from the power supply, P, and the resistance, R, as follows, where I is the current.

$P = V^2/R = I^2 R$ to give V=square root of PR

$R = R_{sp}$ × electrode spacing / current flow area

$R_{sp} = 1400$ kohm·cm

For the AE polysilicon deposition reactor with P = 37 kw and electrode spacing to area ratio of 0.0005 per cm (8m bed height), the required voltage is 5Kvolts. The required current is 7.2 amperes. But to heat the trichlorosilane 100 degrees C, (inlet at 650 °C, bed at 750 °C), we need only 1.31Kvolts. For this more reasonable power requirement, the energy consumption is only 0.66 kw·hr/kg silicon. This value is negligible compared to losses in the distillation towers needed for purification.

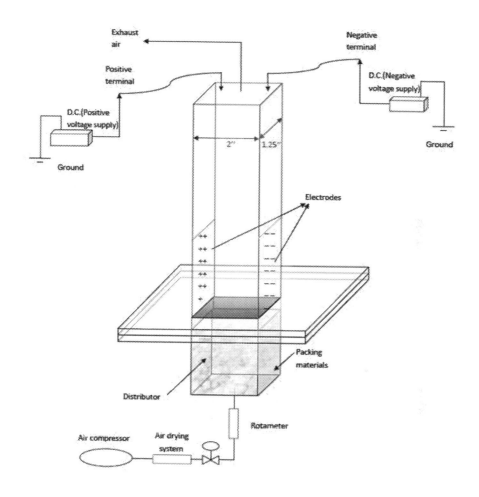

Fig. 3.1 Top: Laboratory experiment

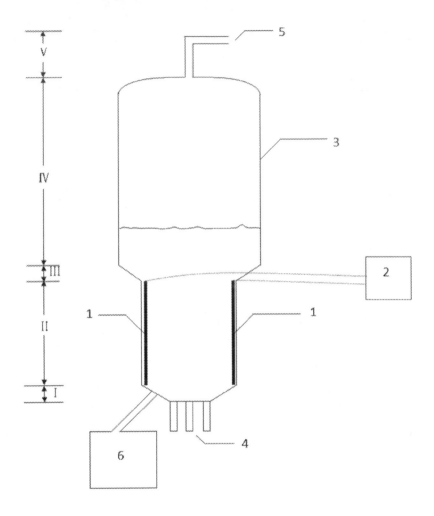

Fig. 3.1 Bottom: Embodiment of an apparatus for the manufacture of high purity polysilicon in a fluidized bed reactor using a novel high voltage heating method

DETAILED DESCRIPTION OF THE PREFERRED EMBODIMENTS

The top of Fig. 3.1 is a laboratory experiment which was used to take data. The bottom of Fig. 3.1 illustrates the embodiment of an apparatus for the manufacture of high purity polysilicon in a fluidized bed reactor using a novel high voltage heating method**1** are silicon electrodes connected by means of wires through the reactor wall to **2**, a variable voltage transformer. **2** steps down the voltage from transmission lines at 110 kilovolts to 10 kilovolts or higher, depending upon the heating demand. The heat is generated in the silicon particles inside the bubbling deposition reactor **3**. The present practice is to heat the deposition reactor using electrical coils wound around the reactor. This conventional method requires the wall to be one hundred degrees hotter than the silicon particles, causing contamination by collision of the silicon particles with the hot, soft wall and restricts the size of the reactor.

The fluidized bed reactor **3** consists of a conical section **I,** a straight tall section **II,** where most of the reaction occurs, another short conical section **III,** an expanded section, **IV,** called a free board, which enhances particle settling and an exit section **V.** Preheated silicon containing gas, $SiHCl_3$ or silane is fed into the conical section through three jcts, marked **4.** A near equilibrium mixture of reactant gases and products containing trapped fines of silicon particles exit pipe **5.** The fines are separated in a cyclone. The silicon fines may be heated, melted and returned as seed particles into the reactor via **4.** The large silicon particles are withdrawn continuously or periodically through a pipe in Section **I** and are stored in the cooler **6** for delivery as the product of the process.

In the fluidized bed reactor pure silicon is produced by thermal decomposition of trichlorosilane by the following chemical reaction:

$$4SiHCl_3(g) = Si\ (s) + 3SiCl_4(g) + 2H_2\ (g)$$

The decomposition occurs on the heated particles of silicon which had been fed into the reactor. There is also decomposition in the gas phase which forms undesirable fines, nanoparticle agglomerates. To suppress the formation of the fines, trichlorosilane is fed into the reactor about 100 degrees C below the decomposition temperature. Based on Mui and Seyferth's [10] final report to JPL on the investigation of the hydrochlorination of silicon tetrachloride and experimental data obtained at AE Polysilicon Corporation, the rate of decomposition, RATE (gmole/cm³·s) is equal to the rate constant, k (1/s) times the difference between the molar silicon concentration of trichlorosilane at any position minus its equilibrium value:

$$RATE = k\ (CSiHCl_3\ CSiHCl_3\ \text{equilbrium})$$

$k = A\ \exp(-E/RT)$
  $A = 1.897 \times 10^{10}$
  $E = 49.9\ kcal/mole$
  $R = 8.314\ kJ/kmole\ K$

At operating temperatures, a high rate of reaction is $RATE = 3 \times 10^{-6}\ gmole/cubic\ cm$-s. In a 4 meter tall reactor filled with seed particles and an effective reaction diameter of 0.1 meters, this rate gives a production of 9.47 kg/hr.

The rate of production of silicon can also be calculated from inflow and outflow trichlorosilane concentrations, since the accumulation is small, as follows:

$$\text{PRODUCTION RATE} = 0.05183\ Avr\ (Y_{inlet} - Y_{outlet})$$

where A is the cross-sectional area, v the velocity, r, the gas density, and Y is the weight fraction of trichlorosilane. As an example, for inlet through 3 jets of 2cm diameter each with an inlet velocity of 10.55m/s at 4.1atm pressure and 623 degrees K, the inlet mass flow rate 411kg/hr. With outlet weight fraction of 0.5, the production rate is 10.7 kg/hr.

The production formula above shows that to maximize production, one needs to operate at higher than atmospheric pressures to increase the gas density and at highest possible velocities. The pressures cannot be too high, since at pressures of, say 20 atm., the reaction will be reversed, as occurs in the production of trichlorosilane from hydrogenation of silicon tetrachloride. In a bubbling bed considered in detail in this invention, the velocities are limited by the terminal velocities of the particles. However, the fluidized bed area can be made as large as desired in this invention. For a large size bed more silicon electrodes will be placed into the reactor than are shown in Figure 1. Hence this invention, teaches both how to produce pure silicon, uncontaminated by the reactor walls and how to make the production rate as large as desired.

A hydrodynamic model and a computer code for the production of silicon with the addition of heat via high voltage heating were developed. The model uses the principle of conservation of mass, momentum and energy for each phase and particle size. Conservation of species equations for the reaction, with the rate described above were programmed into the computational fluid dynamics code described by Dimitri Gidaspow and Veeraya Jiradilok [9].

HYDRODYNAMIC MODEL:

A hydrodynamic model for the production of pure silicon in fluidized bed reactors was developed. It uses the principle of conservation of mass, momentum and energy for each phase. The hydrodynamic models are described in Gidaspow [11] and the computer codes are given in Gidaspow and Jirodilok [9]. Heat is added to the solid particles by means of ε_s QGEN which is generated by the high voltage alternating electric field. QGEN is an input into the code which depends upon the applied voltage.

We used the viscous model to compute the hydrodynamics of silicon particles in a fluidized bed reactor. The equations are the conservation of mass and momentum equations given in Gidaspow [11] as model B. The conservation of species equations were added into the code to describe a consumption of $SiHCl_3$ and production of silicon.

SIMULATION EXAMPLE 1

The hydrodynamic simulation of the production of pure silicon in a fluidized deposition reactor is similar to that described in Gidaspow and Jiradilok [9]. To the hydrodynamic code in the book, conservation of species equations with measured reaction kinetics and conservation of energy equations for the gas and the particles were added. A 10 meter tall, 36 cm wide reactor, experiment with 3 inlet jets, both 2 cm wide, shown in the bottom of Fig. 3.1, is filled with 850 micron silicon seed particles to a height of 230 cm. Trichlorosilane enters the reactor through the jets at a velocity of 655 cm/s at a temperature of 623 degrees Kelvin and a pressure of 4.1 atm.

The reactor wall is maintained at a temperature of 623 degrees Kelvin to prevent corrosion and deposition of silicon on the wall, and yet be hot enough to minimize heat losses. At this low temperature the rate of silicon deposition is zero. In the conventional method of heating the wall temperature must be of the order of 1200 degrees Kelvin to transfer heat to the particles at decomposition temperatures. Here heat is supplied using the two silicon electrodes shown in the bottom of Fig. 3.1. They are connected to a variable voltage transformer which steps down the voltage from transmission lines at 110 kV. The rate of heat generation is 10 watts/cm^3 times the silicon volume fraction. Since the silicon electric conductivity is orders of magnitude higher than that of the gases, only the silicon particles get heated. Hence this method of heating minimizes the thermal decomposition in the gas phase and promotes the growth of silicon particles. In the simulation the initial temperature was set 1023 degrees Kelvin to start the reaction. At first a large bubble filled with the reactant is formed similar to the examples in Gidaspow and Jiradilok [9]. After it breaks, the bed operates in an oscillatory mode, typical of conventional fluidized beds.

Fig. 3.2 shows the axial velocity in the reactor at 48 seconds after start-up. In the center the velocity is about 800 cm/s and smaller in the expanded section. There is the usual down-flow at the walls, needed to keep the particles in the reactor. The high velocity region oscillates with time. Fig. 3.3 shows the solids volume fraction at 48 seconds. There are large elongated bubbles in the bed. The bed expanded to about 550 cm from the initial bed height of 230 cm. With the 3 jets operating at 1055cm/s the bed expands to the top. In the conical section, there is a dense region. But this region is in motion. Such geometry helps the periodic removal of large particles that form in the reactor. Fig. 3.4 shows the particle temperature at 48 seconds. Due to the excellent mixing in fluidized beds, the temperature is nearly constant at about 960 degrees Kelvin. The temperature rises in a very short zone from the inlet of 623 degrees. In the free board the temperature is close to the wall temperature of 623 in the wall region due to poor heat transfer in the absence of particles. With a 50% higher heat input the temperature rises to 1050 K. Fig. 3.5 shows the rate of reaction at 48 seconds. The rate is highest at about 3.5gmole/ $cm^3 \cdot s$ in the center of the reactor. There is no reaction in the wall region. This is an ideal situation. Fig. 3.6 shows the trichlorosilane distribution in the reactor at 48 seconds. It decreases to nearly 40% at the outlet. This gives a production rate of silicon of 40 kg/hr. Fig. 3.7 shows the produced silicon tetrachloride gas at 48 seconds. Due to the high jet velocities there is a central region where there is only the reactant. In the free board we have mostly the product near its equilibrium value.

SIMULATION EXAMPLE 2

Segregation of particles in fluidized bed is a common phenomenon. Gravity causes the large particles to stay at the bottom of fluidized beds, while in packed beds the large particles migrate toward the top. This migration against gravity is called the "Brazil Nut" phenomenon. Quantitative models to describe these phenomena were developed in Gidaspow and Jiradilok [9].

A simulation using a generalization of the hydrodynamic model was used to model a deposition reactor filled with a wide size particle distribution. The same reactor described in Example 1 was used. However, in this example, the bed was filled initially with an equal volume mixture of 550 and 1550 micron size particles. Figs. 3.8 and 3.9 show the computed volume fractions of 1550 and 550 micron size particles at 6 seconds of simulation time, respectively. There is no significant segregation at this high velocity. The bed expansion for the smaller particles is about 30% higher than that for the larger particles. There is no settling except in the cone region. Figure 9 shows cluster formation at the top of the bed at 6 seconds. At 1 second of simulation time, a well-defined bubble for both sizes had formed.

Fig. 3.10 shows the axial velocity of 550 micron silicon particles at 6 seconds. There is violent motion with both up-flow and down-flow. This good mixing leads to the nearly constant temperature shown in Fig. 3.11. Fig. 3.12 shows the rate of reaction at 6 seconds. Similarly to Example 1, the rate of reaction is high in the central region. There is no reaction in the wall region. The differences of the rates of reaction between Fig. 3.5 and Fig. 3.12 are mainly due to their representation at different times. Hence, the production rates of silicon are very similar in both examples. Figs. 13 and 14 show the weight fractions of trichlorosilane and silicon tetrachloride at 6 seconds, respectively. In the central region, there is mostly the reactant trichlorosilane and almost no silicon tetrachloride. However, in this region the formation of silicon is high, as shown in Fig. 3.12. At much lower gas velocities, there is particle segregation and the reactor performance is poor.

REFERENCES

1. Dimitri Gidaspow and Rex T. Ellington, "Surface Combustion of Hydrogen: Part 1.On Platinum Coated Alumina" AIChE Journal 10,No 5,707-713 (1964).
2. Woditisch, Peter and W. Koch, "Solar grade silicon feedstock supply for PV industry" Solar Materials and Solar Cells 72, 11-26 (2002).
3. Ege, Paul, Edward; Hansen, Jeffrey, A. and Allen, Levi, C.," Silicon Spout Fluidized Bed", International Patent Application Number PCT/US2006/028112, International Publication

Number WO 2007/012027 A2, International Publication, date 25 January 2007.

4. Hsu, George, Naresh Rotag and John Houseman, "Silcon Particle Growth in a Fluidized Bed Reactor", AIChE Journal 33. 784-791 May (1987).

5. Poong, Yoon and Song Yongmok, "Method of Preparing a High-Purity Polycrstalline Silicon using a Microwave Heating System in a Fluidized Bed Reactor", US Patent 4,900,411, Feb 13, 1990.

6. Kashyap, Mayank, D. Gidaspow and M. Driscoll, "Effect of Electric Field on the Hydrodynamics of Fluidized Nanoparticles", Powder Technology 183, 441-453 (2008)

7. Tiyapiboonchaiya, Piyawan. S. Damronglerd and D. Gidaspow, "Hydrodynamics of Fluidization with Surface Charge", presented at the AIChE 2010 Annual Meeting, Salt Lake City.

8. Kim, Dae, M.Feng Qian, S.S.Ahmed, H.K. Park and J.L. Sachteng, "Experimental Characteristics of Electrical Conduction in Undoped Polycristalline Silicon Thin Films", Japanese Journal of Applied Physics, Vol. 26, No6, pp863-867, June 1987

9. Dimitri Gidaspow and Veeraya Jiradilok, "Computational Techniques", Nova Science Publishers, 2009.

10. Mui, Jeffrey Y.P. and Dietmar Seyferth, MIT, Cambridge. Ma, "Investigation of the Hydrochlorination of SiCl4" Final report to JPL, Contract No 955 382 (1983).

11. Dimitri Gidaspow, "Multiphase Flow and Fluidization", Academic Press, 1994

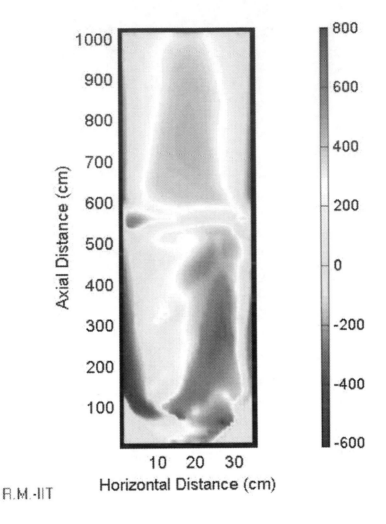

Fig. 3.2. Computed Axial Gas Velocity (cm/s) at 48 Seconds Trichlorosilane enters the reactor through three jets at a velocity of 655 cm/s at a pressure of 4.1 atm.

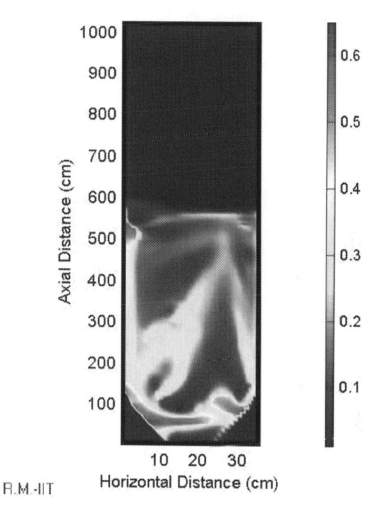

R.M.-IIT

Fig. 3.3. Volume fraction of 850 Micron Silicon Particles at 48 Seconds

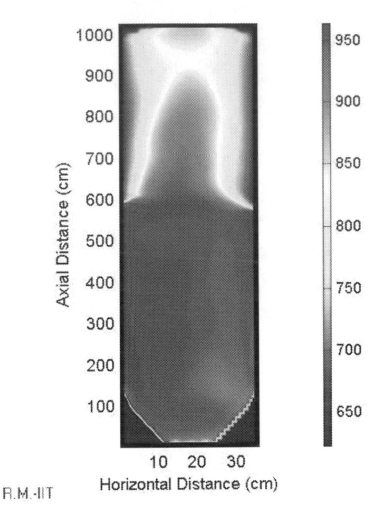

Fig. 3.4. Particle Temperature (K) at 48 Seconds Inlet Gas Temperature = 623 degrees Kelvin Wall Temperature = 623 degrees Kelvin

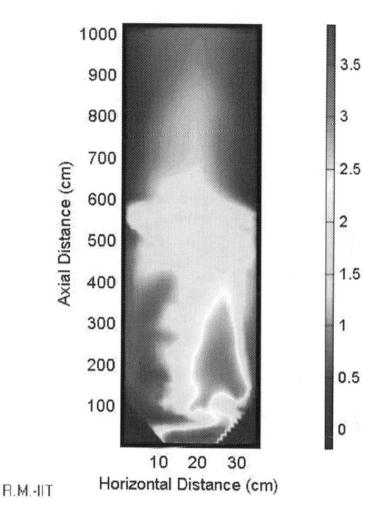

R.M.-IIT

Fig. 3.5. Rate of Reaction ($\times 10^{-6}$ gmole/cm^3·s) at 48 Seconds

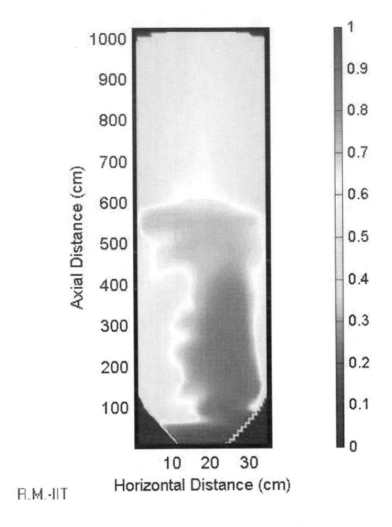

R.M.-IIT

Fig. 3.6. Weight Fraction of Trichlorosilane at 48 Seconds

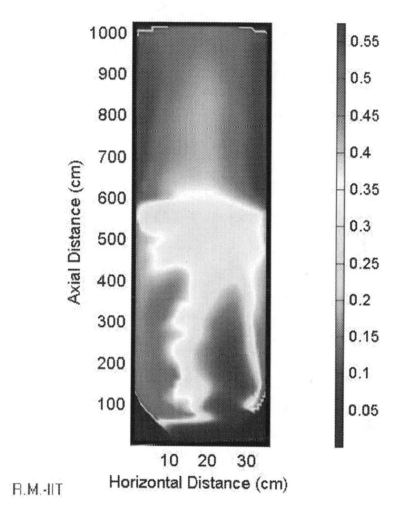

R.M.-IIT

Fig. 3.7. Weight Fraction of SiCl$_4$ at 48 Seconds

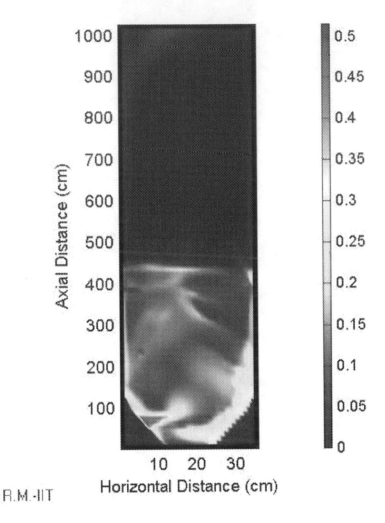

Fig. 3.8. Computed Volume Fraction of 1550 Micron Silicon Particles at 6 Seconds. Equal volume mixture of 550 and 1550 micron particles with three jets entering the reactor at 655 cm/s at temperature of 623 K and a pressure of 4.1 atm. Initial bed height = 230 cm

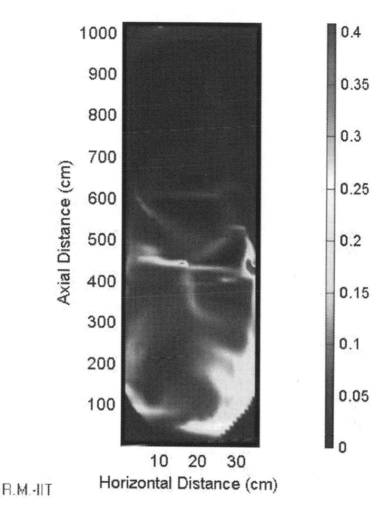

R.M.-IIT

Fig. 3.9. Computed Volume Fraction of 550 Micron Silicon Particles at 6 Seconds. Equal volume mixture of 550 and 1550 micron particles with three jets entering the reactor at 655 cm/s at temperature of 623 K and a pressure of 4.1 atm. Initial bed height = 230 cm

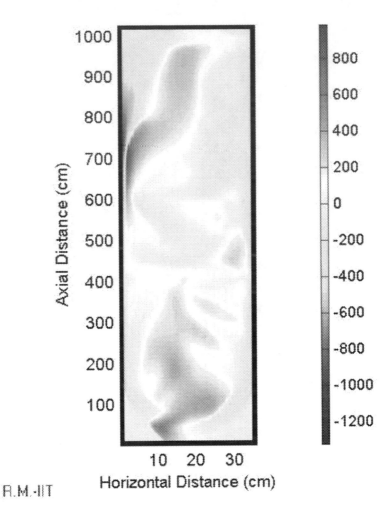

R.M.-IIT

Fig. 3.10. Axial Velocity (cm/s) of 550 Micron Silicon Particles at 6 Seconds

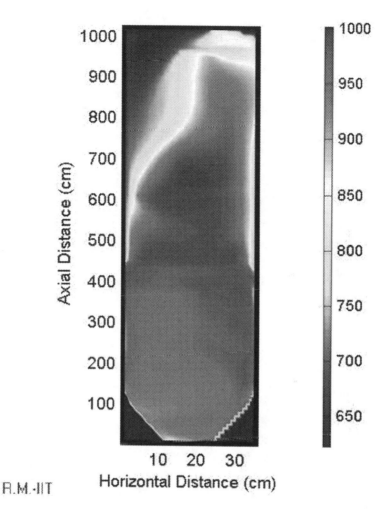

Fig. 3.11. Computed Temperature (K) at 6 Seconds. Inlet Gas
Temperature = 623 degrees Kelvin Wall Temperature = 623 degrees
Kelvin Heat Generation = QGEN = 10 watts/cm^3 of particles

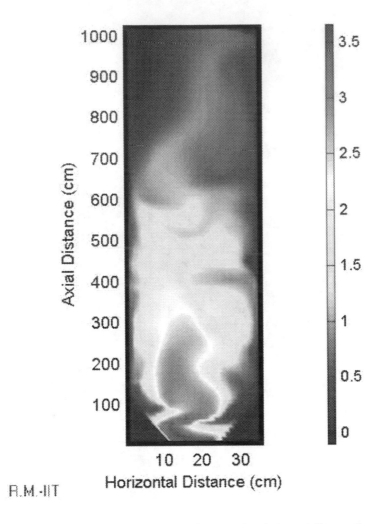

R.M.-IIT

Fig. 3.12. Rate of Reaction ($\times 10^{-6}$ gmole/cm^3·s) at 6 Seconds

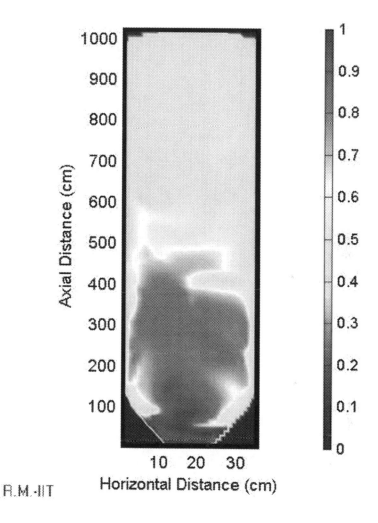

R.M.-IIT

Fig.13. Weight Fraction of Trichlorosilane at 6 Seconds

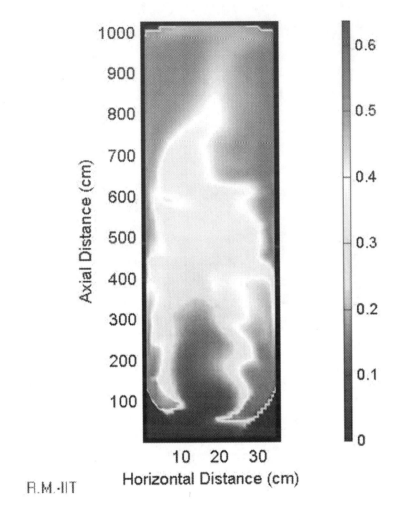

R.M.-IIT

Fig. 3.14. Weight Fraction of SiCl$_4$ at 6 Seconds

4

Alternative Methods of Deriving Multiphase Field Equations

INTRODUCTION

A great deal of theory has arisen over the years concerning multiphase flow modeling. The major thrust in the 1970's and early 1980's was research in the nuclear reactor safety area. Bedford and Drumheller have reviewed this area comprehensively and possibly definitively in their 1983 article which addresses continuum theories of immiscible constituents [1]. This theory constitutes one class of approaches which have been developed to develop multiphase flow equations. In spite of the incredible amount of activity exerted, which subsided significantly beginning in the 1980's because of the Three Mile Island accident which occurred in Pennsylvania on March 28, 1979 and which resulted in the end of nuclear power construction in the United States for decades, not many efforts were pursued coordinating fundamental experimentation and theory. As a result of this oversight, a somewhat less than satisfactory state of affairs persists in the nuclear safety area with unresolved and possibly unresolvable fundamental issues.

In parallel with efforts in the nuclear reactor safety area, indeed primarily independently, slow progress has been made in dry and wet multiphase particulate flow modeling. However, the effort has never been as concentrated nor as directed because a national effort has never materialized. And this is in spite of the efforts of the US Department of Energy (USDOE) to retain America's energy security and international competitiveness. One then wonders whether success can possibly be achieved in this area if the effort is so diffuse. The answer is in the affirmative but only if a coordinated and conscious effort is made to utilize a self-consistent methodology.

Such an effort was initiated in the early 1990's by the USDOE. The Granular Flow Advanced Research Objective (GFARO) was established in 1990 as the first ARO under the auspices of the USDOE Solids Transport Program (STP) funded through the Pittsburgh Energy Technology Center (PETC) [2]. The problem to be addressed by researchers was the flow of dry granular materials in a chute, an area of interest to the US coal industry. There were four focus areas: Theory, Computing, Experimentation, and Instrumentation. The team consisted of two national laboratories, Lawrence Livermore National Laboratory (LLNL) and Sandia National Laboratory (SNL); several universities, and research institutions. A second ARO was proposed to establish what would become known as the Suspension Advanced Research Objective (SARO) to advance the understanding the flow of slurries, suspensions of granular materials in a carrier fluid. Preliminary activities were initiated at Argonne National Laboratory (ANL). The feasibility of applying ANL's water and sodium cooled nuclear reactor instrumentation and experimental research facilities to slurry flows was examined. A literature review of approaches that have been used and/or proposed in the literature to derive multiphase flow equations which would form the basis of the theory and computation of slurries was prepared for the proposed SARO and serves as the basis for the review which constitutes this Chapter. However, this effort was never initiated in spite of strong support by the STP at PETC. PETC was subsequently merged with the Fossil Energy Technology Center (FETC) located in Morgantown West Virginia to form the National Energy Technology Laboratory

(NETL). NETL has picked up the gauntlet to some extent by establishing the annual Workshop on Multiphase Flow Science.

There have been fewer, and possibly only one previous effort which has utilized this philosophy to study wet concentrated suspensions. That is the work of Graham et al. [3, 4, 5] which will be discussed more fully in the section on Statistical Mechanical Theory. This area is of particular interest in the growing area of biological systems and in particular, in the area of hemodynamics transport modeling as described in Chapter 9 of this book and serves to augment Chapters 1 and 2. In briefly, Graham et al. coupled stereoscopic split-screen video determination of three-dimensional particle locations [3] together with techniques derived from Maximum Entropy Principle (MEP), information, and cell theories to determine cluster shape and size distributions [4] and suspension viscosity [5].

We are quite open as to the exact technical formalism which is of most use, but we favor the one that would extend the integral control volume approach based upon individual particle motion developed for dry dense suspensions [6] to provide this framework. The essence of this approach is to apply time-averaging to the integral conservation equations describing discrete particle motion. In this manner, relationships can be established between various terms in the resultant expressions and experimentally measured solids motion using the computer aided particle tracking facility (CAPTF) used at the University of Illinois at Urbana-Champaign by Sun [6]. These include the fluxes, stresses and treatment of the pressure. Yang has also studied this formalism and extended and refined it to some extent. He developed simple models to effect closure [7]. The CAPTF technique has been extended to study the circulation in bubble columns using a single neutrally buoyant radioactive particle [8]. In principle the technique could be used to study wet concentrated suspension flows, however resolution questions arise.

Utilizing the most improved CAPTF, ensemble- and time-averaged solids velocities measured in a thin "two-dimensional" fluidized bed containing a simulated triangular pitch tube array consisting of five round cylinders were analyzed using the hydrodynamic model of fluidization for the first time to these authors' knowledge [9]. Agreement with the solids flow patterns was good, but the magnitude of the maximum velocities differed with the predictions being somewhat higher. The predicted solids velocities in the vicinity of the tubes agreed with inferred solids velocities determined from the power spectra of the pressure fluctuations. The major frequencies predicted from the computer simulation and those obtained from the experiment agreed and lay in a narrow range of 2 to 3 Hz. This type of activity which was planned as a coordinated effort still did not progress as successfully as it could have because of separate funding agencies and the fact the experiments and analysis were done at separate institutions.

Since the extension of this formalism to wet concentrated suspensions wherein the particle and solids densities are comparable has not yet been performed, and which may be fraught with difficulties not yet encountered, we will therefore not be slavish in one recommended formalism. Consequently, we present a concise bird's eye review of alternative approaches that could be used to derive the governing multiphase equations. We claim no attempt at being inclusive, and utilize our considerable experience to guide us in our selection of the pertinent literature assessed. The unique contribution of this review is to intersect these formalisms, and in so doing, effect a synthesis which should advance the understanding of wet dense suspensions. A wide experience is distilled to its essence for the benefit of researchers in this area demanding a clear direction. The viewpoint is therefore somewhat biased; however, hopefully, it is constructively biased.

We concentrate on those references within each formalism which have already been or are being applied to wet dense particulate suspension. These references are briefly critiqued.

The categories of formalisms surveyed include:

1. Continuum theories
2. Statistical Mechanical theories

3. Kinetic Theories of Granular Materials
4. Phenomenological models
5. Discrete Particle Simulators

We will also briefly explain the computer code structure into which the application of the most successful formalism(s) proposed would have been incorporated. The computer code would have utilized the microscopic data taken in a manner as close as possible to the dictates of the formalism(s) and to develop the constitutive and field equations which would be solved to compare macroscopic experimental results with the code predictions. A brief section discusses the status of constitutive relationship modeling and summarizes the most promising formalisms as alternatives/parallel efforts in this SARO. Finally, a few comments are presented concerning future directions.

CONTINUUM THEORIES

A wet concentrated slurry may be viewed as a mixture of immiscible constituents. Immiscibility means that the constituents remain physically separate on a scale which is large in comparison with molecular dimensions. Since the constituents remain physically separated, then it is possible to exploit the fact that, in some local sense, each constituent will obey constitutive relationships for that constituent alone in constructing constitutive relationships for the mixture. Immiscibility also implies the existence of interfaces which separate the constituents. In this light, the review by Bedford and Drumheller [1] and the monograph by Ishii and Hibiki [10], which contains more recent researches into the subject, are relevant.

Bedford and Drumheller [1] single out several works that they consider significant. These are the works of Biot (61-69)[1] for fluid-saturated porous media; Jackson (70), Anderson and Jackson (71, 72), and Murray (73, 74) for fluidized beds; Rudinger and Chang (75),

---

[1] References in parentheses are the ones given in Bedford and Drumheller's 1983 article [1] which the reader is urged to consult since they will not be cited in this chapter.

Panton (76) and Marble (77) for dilute gas-particle flows; and Zuber (78), Soo (78-83), Nigmatulin (84-87), Drew (88, 89) Drew and Segel (90, 91), Ishii (92), and Harlow and Amsden (93) for multiphase flow.

Bedford and Drumheller [1] review the classical continuum theory of mixtures which is a nice formalism but for which little if any comparisons with data have ever been performed. This formalism is basically dead-ended, fruitless and misleading since early on, it gave researchers the impression it could be used for multiphase flows, which it cannot. The remaining theories are broken down into:

1. some theories with microstructure.
2. volume fraction theories, postulated,
3. volume fraction theories, averaged,
4. theories having greater microstructure content, and
5. theories for composite materials.

The volume fraction (sometimes referred to as interpenetrating continua) theories reviewed by Bedford and Drumheller [1] are particularly relevant. These include the section on fluidized beds (postulational) and averaging techniques. The controversial issues concerning the added mass and treatment of the pressure terms persist It is clear that the final form of these terms are not the result of averaging processes. The added mass is postulational and the pressure treatment goes to a point where postulates take over to effect closure.

The theories using time- and/or volume-averaging are reviewed. Major contributors cited are Ishii (61) (time-averaging); Anderson and Jackson (71), Murray (73), and Nigmatulin (87) (volume-averaging); and Delhaye (235-238) (time- and volume-averaging). Notably lacking is any reference to the work of Whitaker ([11], for example), Slattery ([12], for example) or Gray ([13], for example), possibly because these authors publish in the chemical and civil engineering literature. The averaging approach offers us a template, which we refer to as the "basic" equations, i.e., a major portion of the "left side" of the governing field equations. The integrals in the general partial-differential-integral equations must be evaluated, approximated, or modeled to effect closure. This is the general framework which has evolved into the formalism we are considering begun by Sun [6] and Yang [7]. The variational theory of Bedford and Drumheller (162-163) was noted and applied by Hill et al. (212) to describe batch sedimentation of whole human blood agreeing quite well with experimental data. Since sedimentation involves dense wet suspensions, this theory should be considered as a possible candidate.

Syamlal and O'Brien [14] extended the hydrodynamic theory of fluidization (see Lyczkowski et al. [9], for example) to multi-particles. They applied the model to simulate granular layer inversion in a liquid fluidized bed. The phenomenon occurs during the fluidization of a binary mixture of particles in which the denser particles are smaller. In such a system, at low fluid velocities, the larger particles segregate into a top layer. At higher fluid velocities, they sink to form a bottom layer. The simulations were in good agreement with experimental data for granular layer inversion. They also showed that under some conditions, a radial segregation pattern exists in addition to the experimentally observed axial segregation pattern. They concluded that the good agreement with data lent increased confidence in the inter-particle and fluid-solids drag terms and buoyancy effects. However, further development of the constitutive models for solids pressure and particle-particle interactions is needed.

Gidaspow et al. [15] developed a theory to describe quantitatively the sedimentation of colloidal particles in vessels having electrodes that are inclined to the vertical. These devices are called lamella electrosettlers and are used to remove fine particles from suspensions which would not otherwise settle out. They predicted motions and settling fronts and the thickness of the clear boundary layers which formed, to globally agree with experimental data.

STATISTICAL MECHANICAL HEORIES

Buyevich (231, 232) used a statistical approach to the problem of averaging. According to Bedford and Drumheller [1] the method is suspected of being severely limited as to the range of applicability due to his estimates of quantities characterizing random local motion of the phases.

Graham and Steele [4] reconstructed the probability distribution of cluster sizes of uniform diameter spheres in what they considered concentrated suspensions subjected to homogeneous shear flow by combining experimental data [3] with techniques derived from the MEP and information theory. They found the average cluster size to increase rapidly and nonlinearly as the volume concentration of solids increases. They also found the average cluster size to decrease slightly and the size distribution to become more random as the rate of shear increases. They felt that the procedure utilized provided the least-biased estimate of the distribution of all the particles in clusters of various sizes on the basis of partial information. They recommended, however, that more data be taken over a wider range of solids volume fraction and particle Reynolds numbers and for a wider variety of flows and fluids to further understand the dynamic structure in suspensions. They studied solids volume fractions up to 0.2 and particle Reynolds numbers up to 700. Graham et al. [5] were then able to use the cluster information to predict the viscosity of the suspension. This study is a good example of a coordinated research effort utilizing a self-consistent methodology for data acquisition, data analysis and application. The same data, or data of its type can be used with the extended Sun [6] formalism to produce terms and constitutive relationships in the field equations. Yang [7] proposed a similar formalism using laser doppler velocimetry (LDV) measurements of solids motion.

KINETIC THEORIES OF GRANULAR MATERIALS

de Groot and Mazur present a concise discussion of the Kinetic Theory of Gases in their classic text [16] to which the reader is referred for background information concerning the basic concepts and the complex mathematics of this formalism. Syamlal [17] and Gidaspow [18] review the applications of the Kinetic Theory formalism to the flow of granular materials. They both combined the Kinetic Theories of Granular flow with the continuum theory of fluidization. Syamlal [17] recommended the theory of Lun et al. [19] for computational purposes for dry fluidized beds since the collision effects there are quite important. Both Syamlal [17] and Gidaspow [18] agree that Bagnold [20] probably began the Kinetic Theory of Granular Flow in 1954 using very primative expressions for the collision frequency of particles. Syamlal [17] recommended a two-step approach to developing the theory further:

1. perform computations using an approximate solution for the fluctuation velocity, and
2. after gaining confidence in this simpler version of the theory, the equation of random motion kinetic energy (usually referred to as the granular temperature equation [18]) can be combined with the model to determine the fluctuation velocity and, hence, the granular stress.

Syamlal has not progressed beyond the first step. However, Ding and Gidaspow [21] went directly to the second step. Gidaspow [18] has extended the Ding and Gidaspow model. In this form it may be applicable for wet as well as dry dense suspension flows.

The advantage of the Kinetic Theory of Granular materials is that it provides a priori estimates of the solids viscosities and pressure. In the case of uniform granular temperature, the momentum equations reduce to the Navier Stokes equations assumed in the continuum theories.

Thus far, only binary collisions between particles have been considered but advances on this front are progressing ([22], for example). The effects of the interstitial fluid have also been investigated [23].

PHENOMENOLOGICAL MODELS

Phenomenological models of dense suspension, usually called slurries, are extensions of so-called non-Newtonian fluid models. Skelland [24] and Bird et al. [25] are good sources for these models which include the power-law, Ellis, and Bingham fluid models. To apply these models to a dense suspension from single-phase formulations requires some assumptions. The usual assumptions are that the concentration is uniform and that there is zero slip between the phases. This is the homogeneous flow model which uses the mixture velocity in the various non-Newtonian flow models. Roco and Shook [26] and Soo [27] were probably among the first to develop steady-state phenomenological models taking into account concentration and relative motion effects. Roco and Shook [26] show good agreement with concentration and velocity profiles.

Lyczkowski and Wang [28] extended the non-Newtonian power-law model to describe the solids rheology for nonhomogeneous slurry flow. The model developed predicts two-dimensional spatial and temporal variations of solids and liquid velocities and concentrations. Comparisons with analytical solutions and capillary tube viscometer shear rate, viscosity, mass flow and pressure drop served to validate the new model. It was concluded that further validation is required especially at very high shear rates (greater than 40,000 s⁻¹), wider range of solids loadings, different sample materials under steady-state, and transient conditions.

DISCRETE PARTICLE SIMULATORS

In this formalism, rules of various kinds are formulated to account for the interactions and movements of pieces of fluid or particles treated either as points, circles or spheres. The work of Walton [29] is especially to be singled out since he has had a continuous effort in this area for well over ten years. Walton's simulators have advanced to the stage where the calculations can be compared with results from the Kinetic Theory of Granular Flow for dry dense suspensions. The agreement with the theories and data are encouraging.

Brady and Bossis [30] reviewed the dynamic simulator method. They categorized these dynamic simulators into five types depending upon the length scale on which the phenomena are represented.

1. molecular scale. This category entails the conventional molecular dynamics. Newton's equations of motion are simulated with particles in a vacuum interacting through Lennard-Jones, hard-sphere, electrostatic, and various other types of interparticle forces.
2. macromolecule level. Here the intramolecular structure is simulated using information on bond distances and angles.
3. Stokesian dynamics. At this level materials such as polymer molecules, larger colloidal particles, glass beads, fibers, and coal particles, for example are dispersed in a continuum. The problem now dictates that changes in the structure are dictated by continuum-scale interparticle forces, such as London-van der Waals, electrostatic, and hydrodynamic forces transmitted via the intervening continuum fluid. Here, the basic assumption is that the particle Reynolds number is small and that their motion is governed by Stokes equations.
4. granular dynamics. At this level we are dealing with materials such as sand grains, seeds, billiard balls and the like. While governed by a continuum scale, it is assumed that the fluid, usually air, separating the grains plays nor role, i.e. high Reynolds number flows. Collisional interactions predominate. This is the area where Walton [29] has contributed as noted above. Brady and Bossis [30] consider this to be a fascinating new area of dynamic simulation.
5. stellar dynamics. Here, planets, stars or entire galaxies of stars are treated as point masses and interact through a vacuum according to Newton's law of gravity.

Brady and Bossis [30] have contributed to the third category above with a new molecular-dynamics-like approach which they call Stokesian dynamics. The claims are rather broad. Both hydrodynamic and nonhydrodynamic forces are considered. Both static and dynamic micro-structural properties, as well as macroscopic properties in either dilute or concentrated are claimed to be capable of being treated.

Brady and Bossis [30] studied the shear viscosity of a monolayer of identical spheres oriented perpendicular to the walls. The area fraction of particles used was 0.4 and 49 particles were employed in the simulation. They found very large fluctuations in the suspension viscosity and attributed them to the formation and breakup of clusters. When the clusters spanned the distance between the walls, the viscosity increased. The removal of even one sphere in the connectivity caused the viscosity to drop by a factor of four. At a particle area ratio of 0.6, plug-flow behavior was noted. In this regime, the cluster moved more or less as a single entity.

Brady and Bossis [30] concluded that in concentrated suspensions, the cluster formation seems to be the most important aspect controlling the behavior. They further conclude that the simulation method they developed provides a rigorous and accurate procedure for dynamically simulating hydrodynamically interacting particles and suspensions. Its utility is presently limited by computer storage requirements, but with the advancement of parallel processor computers, this obstacle may be overcome.

Finally, a word must be said for the lattice gas automaton approach. Hassler [31] has reviewed this subject which resembles the Monte Carlo technique for heat transfer. A set of rules are assigned to the particles which interact with each other. Very realistic simulations have been performed in two- and three-dimensions. The technique has been extended to model granular materials [32]. The entire area is very new and potentially useful, however, the subject is really in its infancy.

COMPUTATIONAL FRAMEWORK

In order to realize the goals of the SARO that was proposed, we would have utilized the computer program FLUFIX [33] which formed the basis of the SLUFIX computer program [28]. FLUFIX is a pilot scale transient two-dimensional computer program which uses the two-fluid hydrodynamic model for application to fluid-flow simulation in fluid-solids systems. In a collaborative effort with Babcock & Wilcox, the three-dimensional FORCE2 computer code has been developed [34]. FORCE2 is a transient and steady-state, finite control volume, industrial grade and quality embodiment of the pilot scale FLUFIX including a distributed resistance model, and surface and volume porosities representing embedded solid structures.

We implemented the FLUFIX and FORCE2 computer programs on Argonne National Laboratories' Cray X-MP/14 vector supercomputer and performed quality assurance and validation using some of the experimental results from the Illinois Institute of Technology [18]. Good agreement of the computed overall solids flow patterns, major porosity and pressure frequencies, bubble sizes and frequencies and time-averaged porosity profiles with experimental data has been achieved (see references [9], [18], and [28] for example).

Advanced graphics have been implemented with the assistance of ANL's Scientific Visualization Facility (SVF) staff. These advanced graphics serve to speed up the validation process and to render the computer simulations more comprehensible to the users of the FLUFIX computer program.

UNRESOLVED ISSUES FOR KEY CONSTITUTIVE RELATIONSHIPS AND RECOMMENDED FORMALISMS

The weakest links in the continuum theories are the models for the solids pressure and the inclusion of terms to cause solids to migrate out of regions of very high shear. The proper forms of the solids pressure to account for particle diameter and multi-particle effects are not known. In principle the Multiphase Kinetic Theory of Granular

Materials can supply these expressions, but the extension of the theories to multiple particles is in its infancy [35]. A hybrid theory needs to be developed taking the most salient portion of the continuum models and the Multiphase Kinetic Theory Models. Comparison of Kinetic Theory calculations using the Ding and Gidaspow [21] model with the basic continuum model calculations have been performed for the sample problem described in the FLUFIX [33] document. Away from the obstacle, results are practically identical. Near the obstacle in the region of very high shear, neither theory agrees particularly well with the time-averaged porosity. This leads us to conjecture that a term taking into account particle rotation resembling the Magnus force [36] should be added. This term may be crucial to predict the clear layer which form at the wall of the tube for intermediate shear rates. The work of Givler [37] may be useful for the solids pressure term at the low Reynolds number flows typically encountered for dense suspensions

CLOSING COMMENTS

The fact that two completely independent methodologies, Graham et al. [3-5] and Brady and Bossis [30)] concluded that cluster formation is **the** key to dense supension behavior is a significant finding. Neither set of investigators was aware of the others work. If the cluster formation is the key to understanding wet dense suspensions, we are fortunate. This means that instead of resolving motion of individual particle motion experimentally, we only need to resolve down to the cluster size which, at a solids volume fraction of 0.2 is a consisting of roughly 6 particles[4] The work of Brady and Bossis [30] suggests that these clusters become string-like or even plug-flow-like at higher suspension solids fractions. The questions remains as to whether this is a blessing or a curse. Fortunately, the continuum hyd|rodynamic theory has already computed clusters which have been conjectured to play an important role in gas fluidized beds [38].

An excellent adjunct to this review which complements it was presented by Sankaran Sundaresan at the 10TH International

Conference on Circulating Fluidized Beds and Fluidization Technology- CFB-10 [39].

REFERENCES

1. Bedford, A. and D. S. Drumheller, *Theories of Immiscible and Structured Mixtures,* Int. J. Eng. Sci., 21, pp. 863-960 (1983).
2. Passman, Stephen L. and William C. Peters, *United States Department of Energy Granular Flow Advanced Research Objective*, SAND92-0069 (DE93 006447) (Nov. 1992).
3. Graham, A. L. and R. B. Bird, *Particle Clusters in Concentrated Suspensions. 1. Experimental Observations of Particle Clusters,* Ind. Eng. Chem. Fund., 23, pp. 406-410 (1984).
4. Graham, A. L. and R. D. Steele. *Particle Clusters in Concentrated Suspensions. 2. Information Theory and Particle Clusters.* 23, pp. 411-420 (1984).
5. Graham, A. L., R. D. Steele and R. B. Bird, *Particle Clusters In Concentrated Suspensions. 3. Prediction of Suspension Viscosity,* 23, pp. 420-425 (1984).
6. Sun, J. G., *Analysis of Solids Dynamics and Heat Transfer in Fluidized Beds,* Chapter 3, Ph. D. Dissertation, University of Illinois at Urbana Champaign, Department of Mechanical and Industrial Engineering (1989).
7. Yang, Y., *Experiments and Theory on Gas-Cohesive Particles Two-Phase Flow and Agglomeration in the Fluidized Bed,* Ph.D. Thesis Proposal, Department of Chemical Engineering, Illinois Institute of Technology (March, 1991).
8. Moselman, D., N. Devanathan and M. P. Dudukovic, *Liquid Circulation in Bubble Columns Via the CARPTF Facility Effects of Superficial Gas Velocity and Column Diameter,* paper presented at the International Symposium on Gas-Liquid Two Phase Flows, ASME Winter Annual Meeting, Dallas TX, Nov. 25-30, 1990 (1990).

9. Lyczkowski, R.W., I.K. Gamwo, F. Dobran, Y.H. Ai, B.T. Chao, M.M. Chen, and D. Gidaspow, *Validation of Computed Solids Hydrodynamics and Pressure Oscillations in a Model Bubbling Atmospheric Fluidized Bed Combustor*, Powder Technology, 76, No. 1, 65-77 (July 1993).

10. Ishii, Mamoru and Takashi Hibiki, *Thermo-Fluid Dynamics of Two-Phase Flow Second Edition*, Springer, New York (2011).

11. Whitaker, S., *Advances in Theory of Fluid Motion in Porous Media,* Industrial and Engineering Chemistry, 61, No. 12, pp. 14-28 (Dec, 1969).

12. Slattery, J. C, *Flow of Viscoelastic Fluids Through Porous Media,* AIChE Journal, 13, pp. 1066-1071 (1967).

13. Gray, W. G., *A Derivation of the Equations for Multi-Phase Transport,* Chem. Eng. Sci., 30, pp. 229-233 (1975).

14. Syamlal, M. and T. J. O'Brien, *Simulation of Granular Layer Inversion In Liquid Fluidized Beds,* Int. J. Multiphase Flow, 14, No. 4, pp. 473-481 (1988).

15. Gidaspow, D., Y.-T. Shih, J. X. Bouillard and D. T. Wasan, *Hydrodynamics of a Lamella Electrosettler,* AIChE Journal, 35, No. 5, pp. 714-724 (1989).

16. de Groot, S. R. and P. Mazur, *Non-Equilibrium Thermodynamics,* Chapter IX, Dover Publications, Inc., New York (1984).

17. Syamlal, Madhava *A Review of Granular Stress Constitutive Relations,* EG&G Washington Analytical Services Technical Report DOE/MC/21353-2372, Morgantown, WV, available from NTIS, Springfield, VA, DE87006499 (Jan., 1987).

18. Gidaspow, D. *Multiphase Flow and Fluidization Continuum and Kinetic Theory Descriptions,* Chapter 9. Kinetic Theory Approach, Academic Press, San Diego (1994).

19. Lun, C. K. K., S. B. Savage, D. J. Jeffrey, and N. Chepurbiy, *Kinetic Theories for Granular Flow:Inelastic Particles in Couette Flow and Slightly Inelastic Particles in a General Flowfield,* J. Fluid. Mech., 140, pp. 223-256 (1984).

20. Bagnold, R. A., *Experiments on a Gravity-Free Dispersion of Large Solid Spheres in a Newtonian Fluid Under Shear,* Arch. Mech., A225, pp. 49-63 (1954).

21. Ding, J. and D. Gidaspow, *A Bubbling Fluidization Model Using Kinetic Using Kinetic Theory of Granular Flow,* AIChE Journal, 36, No. 4, pp. 523-538 (1990).

22. Jenkins, J. T. and F. Mancini, *Kinetic Theory for Binary Mixtures of Smooth, Nearly Elastic Spheres,* Phys. Fluids, A1, pp. 2050-2057 (1989).

23. Ma, D. and G. Ahmadi, *A Kinetic Theory for Rapid Granular Flows of Nearly Elastic Particles Including Interstitial Fluid Effects,* Powder Technology, 56, pp. 191-207 (1988).

24. Skelland, A. H. P., *Non-Newtonian Flow and Heat Transfer,* John Wiley & Sons, Inc. (1967).

25. Bird, R. B., R. C. Armstrong, and O. Hassager, *Dynamics of Polymeric Liquids Volume 1 Fluid Mechanics,* John Wiley & Sons, New York (1977).

26. Roco, M. C, and C. A. Shook, *Modeling of Slurry Flow. The Effect of Particle Size,* Canadian Journal of Cmeical Engineering, 6_i, pp. 494-503 (1983).

27. Soo, S. L., *Pipe Flow of a Dense Suspension,* Journal of Pipelines, 6, pp. 193-203 (1987).

28. Lyczkowski, R. W. and C. S. Wang, *Hydrodynamic Modeling and Analysis of Two-Phase Non-Newtonian Coal/Water Slurries,* Powder Technology, 69, pp. 285-294 (1992).

29. Walton, O. R., *Understanding Particulate Flow Behavior,* The LLNL Quarterly, Lawrence Livermore National Laboratory, Livermore, CA (Sept., 1988).

30. Brady, J. F. and G. Bossis, *Stokesian Dynamics,* in Annual Reviews of Fluid Mechanics, 20, pp. 111-157(1988).

31. Hassler, B., *Discrete Fluids,* Los Alamos Science Special Issue, pp. 175-200 (1987).

32. Gutt, G. M. and P. K. Haff, *Lattice Gas Models of Flowing Granular Materials,* presented at Joint DOE/NSF Workshop on Fluid-Solids Transport, Pleasanton, CA (May, 1989).

33. Lyczkowski, R.W., J.X. Bouillard, and S.M. Folga, *Users Manual for FLUFIX/MOD2: A Computer Program for Fluid-Solids Hydrodynamics*, Argonne National Laboratory Sponsor Report, Argonne, IL (April 1992). Reprinted by USDOE METC as DOE/MC/24193-3491/NTIS no. DE94000033), available from NTIS, Springfield, VA (1994).

34. S.W. Burge, R.W. Lyczkowski, and J.X. Bouillard, *FORCE2*. Software package submitted June 1994. ESTSC Package IB – 000722SUN0000.

35. Gidaspow, D. and V. Jiradilok, *Computational Techniques: The Multiphase CFD Approach to Fluidization and Green Energy Technologies*, Nova Science Publishers Inc., New York (2009).

36. Torvik, R. and H. F. Svendsen, *Modeling of Slurry Reactors: A Fundamental Approach*, Chemical Engineering Science, 45, No. 8, pp. 2325-2332 (1990).

37. Givler, R. C, *An Interpretation For the Solid-Phase Pressure In Slow, Fluid-Particle Flows*, International Journal of Multiphase Flow, 13, No. 5, pp. 717-722 (1987).

38. Gidaspow, D., Y. P. Tsuo and K. M. Luo, *Computed and Experimental Cluster Formalin and Velocity Profiles In Circulating Fluidized Beds*, in Fluidization VI, Proceedings of the International Conference on Fluidization, J. R. Grace, L. W. Shemilt and M. A. Bergougnou, eds., pp. 81-88, Engineering Foundation, New York (1989).

39. Sundaresan, Sankaran, *Reflections on Mathematical Models and Simulation of Gas-Particle Flows* in "10th International Conference on Circulating Fluidized Beds and Fluidization Technology- CFB-10", T. Knowlton, Ed., ECI Symposium Series, (2013). http://dc.engconfintl.org/cfb10/2